Jane Austen's
Heroines

Jane Austen's Heroines

Intimacy in human relationships

John Hardy

Routledge & Kegan Paul
London and New York

First published in 1984
by Routledge & Kegan Paul Ltd.

11 New Fetter Lane, London EC4P 4EE

Published in the USA by
Routledge and Kegan Paul Inc.
in association with Methuen Inc.
29 West 35th Street, New York NY10001

Set in Bembo 11 on 13 point
by Set Fair Ltd., London
and printed in Great Britain
by Thetford Press Ltd., Thetford, Norfolk

Library of Congress Cataloging in Publication Data

Hardy, J. P. (John P.), 1933–

Jane Austen's heroines.
Includes Index.
1. Austen, Jane, 1775-1817—Characters—Heroines.
2. Austen, Jane, 1775-1817—Knowledge—Psychology.
3. Heroines in literature. 4. Intimacy (Psychology) in
literature. 5. Interpersonal relations in literature.
I. Title.
PR4038.H4H37   1985   823'.7   84-8234

British Library CIP Data available

ISBN 0 7102 1118 X

TO CATHIE

Contents

Acknowledgements

I am pleased to acknowledge the assistance of the Australian Research Grants Scheme in the preparation of this book. I have also been greatly helped by two people: Nicholas Brown, my research assistant, who has contributed much more to it than he would acknowledge; and Dallas de Brabander, who did a splendid job in typing the final draft. To both of them I wish to express my sincere thanks. I am also indebted to John Burrows for providing me with a print-out from his recently compiled Concordance.

Quotations from the novels, with page references given in brackets, are taken from the Oxford edition of *The Novels of Jane Austen*, edited by R. W. Chapman and revised by Mary Lascelles. For convenience of reference, I have in the notes cited wherever possible two collections of Austen criticism. Both have been edited by B. C. Southam and are indicated by the following abbreviated titles: *Casebook 1, Jane Austen: 'Sense and Sensibility', 'Pride and Prejudice' and 'Mansfield Park': A Casebook*, London, Macmillan, 1976, and *Casebook 2, Jane Austen: 'Northanger Abbey' and 'Persuasion': A Casebook*, London, Macmillan, 1976.

Introduction

Elizabeth Hardwick has sounded a warning to anyone writing a book on Jane Austen: 'One thing, I think, we may surely say . . . is that she is much more fun to read than to read about.'[1] While this is also true of other great writers, it is, perhaps, particularly apt as a comment on Austen. Seemingly it has proved difficult to capture what is quintessential about her work, a good deal of criticism having failed to do it justice. In this respect we are reminded of Virginia Woolf's words: 'Of all great writers she is the most difficult to catch in the act of greatness.'[2]

The attempt to do this has most often resulted in what has been called (and challenged as) 'the prevailing view of Austen as a cool, rational comedienne of manners who delineates social surfaces and measures comic aberrations against the stable moral norms of a civilisation in whose values she has supreme confidence'.[3] Such a view rests too easily in externals. It is not merely question-begging in terms of the 'values' it assumes, but it deflects consideration away from Austen's subtle and original portrayal of her heroines. The unsympathetic modern reader may show irritation at a seemingly irrelevant set of old-fashioned conventions, but the discerning reader can surely be encouraged to see what these become a background or vehicle for – almost a unique insight into what is of central importance in human relationships.

The Austen heroine comes to enjoy a distinctive

relationship with the man she eventually marries. Though this is handled differently from novel to novel, an essential element is the potential, at least, that exists for the kind of intimacy which involves a mutual recognition of the other person and leads to a shared privacy.[4] Whatever the latent feeling on each side, or the fascination indicating that something has caught between two people, there is above all the need to acknowledge and respond to the other person. Without this degree of personal and moral awareness, there could only be such a compromising and submerging of the self as would be inimical to the development of real intimacy.

This point has been variously touched on (without ever being realised in precisely these terms) by several of Austen's readers. It has been suggested, for example, either that the heroine's 'development' must be understood 'not in our modern sense of change and becoming but in the older sense of discovery or disclosure',[5] or that 'Jane Austen has greater faith than most writers in the love fully combined with knowledge of self and esteem for the partner that is implied in her version of the pedagogic relationship'.[6] Yet such formulations, however partially useful, do not sufficiently bring out how the heroine's individual awareness is essential to her recognition of another, or even the peculiarly eager and vibrant responsiveness that flows from this. It is here that Jane Austen shows herself most penetratingly in touch with human nature, and with one means by which the inherently conflicting claims of public and private can be willingly reconciled.

It has recently been shown that, together with Mary Wollstonecraft, Jane Austen inherited 'a common tradition of feminist development'.[7] In the moral intelligence she imparts to her heroines, their individuality is stressed through the quality of their interaction with others. As well as remaining true to inner feelings and perceptions, they have the ability of acknowledging the legitimate claims of others. Generosity is an important attribute here. So too is self-command, or the virtue (to borrow Coleridge's phrase) of 'steady self-possession'.[8] What is important is the capacity of being collected within the self, but disinterestedly so, in order that the potential always exists of responding to others.

That Jane Austen explores human relationships at this depth means that her heroines at some stage seem more alone or isolated than many of her minor characters. While it has been claimed that the 'theme of isolation' in the novels gives expression to 'the essential loneliness of men and women',[9] none of the heroines ends up alone. Nor is this dictated merely by the convention of a happy ending. Rather it follows from those qualities of mind and heart which enable a process of mutual sharing to occur between two people. In this sense the heroine's isolation admits of a genuine resolution – one that invigorates and is not just consoling.[10] Indeed, Jane Austen was firmly in possession of the truth about human existence which Nicolas Berdyaev has reminded us of, namely, that 'love and friendship are man's only hope of triumphing over solitude'.[11] Moreover, she turns this perception to her own advantage in that there exists a connection (not always easy to elaborate or explain) between the heroine's being thrown on her own resources and the kind or quality of character that this experience refines or reveals. Whatever the means employed, what remains distinctive about her heroines is their active involvement in the situations in which they find themselves. Though they may be isolated, they are never static or inert, for all are engaged in a continuous, ongoing activity of thinking and responding. Not only does this fact lift the moral seriousness of the novels far above the prescriptions of the conduct books (whose vocabulary they partly inherit); it also represents their distinctive advance on earlier English fiction. The satisfaction we feel in reading Jane Austen stems from the heroines' right to find happiness because of the kind of people they are – because of their integrity towards themselves and others.

Catherine Morland is arguably the least sophisticated of Jane Austen's heroines, yet her very openness almost guarantees Henry Tilney's corresponding interest in her 'fresh feelings of every sort'. Elinor Dashwood, too, like Catherine, has a certain integrity of self that allows her to feel for Edward Ferrars when she is seemingly cut off from him. This ensures that, given happier circumstances, the potential exists between them for a process of mutual sharing, and our most vivid intimation of this is the suggestion that no conversation between them as 'lovers' can ever really be 'finished'.[12] Elizabeth Bennet's vivacity captivates Fitzwilliam Darcy and draws him close to her even though she seeks to make him dislike her. Theirs becomes a tantalising process of sharing even before it is recognised as such. Fanny Price is always disposed to give herself unstintingly to Edmund Bertram, but *Mansfield Park*, of all the novels, seems to suffer from a thwarting of such intimacy through Edmund's preoccupation with Mary Crawford and the spurious kind of intimacy which Henry Crawford seeks to establish with Fanny. Emma Woodhouse takes even longer than Elizabeth to perceive how her heart is engaged. While her incipient interest in Mr Knightley (as well as his intense interest in her) is clear almost from the beginning, her sense of this is obscured by an energy that seeks to create for itself more ready-made, even vicarious, objects of interest. Anne Elliot never has any doubt of her feelings for the previously rejected Captain Wentworth, though she cannot herself be sure what he is feeling. Communication between them is therefore agonisingly delayed – until, that is, their renewed intimacy can be enriched by sharing what each has felt and suffered in the long interval of estrangement.

What catches between the heroines and the men they come to marry is not themselves in any abstract sense, but their very beings as defined by their characters and their whole personalities. As Erich Fromm has reminded us, 'love is not primarily "caused" by a specific object, but a lingering quality in a person which is only actualized by a certain "object".'[13] In Jane Austen's world, such a 'quality' does not exist capriciously, independent of other qualities that define the individual self. And this 'quality' (or these qualities) is (or are) most fully manifested in the mutual sense of attraction that flows between two people. What is involved is not merely mutual respect (which is all Sir Thomas and Lady Bertram seem left with), but such mutual responsiveness as guarantees that the conversation between lovers will never have an ending. The manner, then, should not obscure what is of central interest in the novels – which D. H. Lawrence overlooked when he slighted Jane Austen for being an 'old maid' who 'typifies . . . the sharp knowing in apartness instead of knowing in togetherness'.[14] Our author's treatment of sex (which is certainly not sexist) operates in a different mode. Nor does this mean that she is any less clear-sighted about the things that draw people together. Indeed, her perception of these is such as to allow her heroines both fascination and dignity.

Catherine Morland

Northanger Abbey was arguably the first of Jane Austen's novels to be substantially completed in its present form. Its heroine Catherine Morland marks a distinct break with the earlier type of heroine she burlesqued in her juvenilia. Even though the undercutting in the first two chapters might seem at first glance to be directed against Catherine, a more careful reading shows its primary target to be the conventional sentimental heroine whose life proved so 'eventful' (15). In her new kind of fiction, Jane Austen subtly counterpoints former extravagances to imply how ineffectual these are in comprehending the more important vagaries of ordinary life. Despite Catherine's seemingly unpromising start and lack of prospects, her life does become eventful. Not only does she meet a lover in Henry Tilney, but an anticipation of something 'very shocking', 'horrible', and 'uncommonly dreadful' (112) is fulfilled in what happens to her (though not in the sense in which she originally understands these words). Mrs Allen, with whom she goes to Bath, is not the treacherous chaperon of eighteenth-century fiction who will be guilty of turning her 'out of doors' (20). Instead this is reserved for her future father-in-law General Tilney.

Early in the second chapter the assumed normalcy of Catherine's world is clear from the preparations for her journey that her family makes 'with a degree of moderation and composure, which seemed rather consistent with the common feelings of common life' (19). Jane Austen's

1

description of her heroine is similarly without heightening:

> Her heart was affectionate, her disposition cheerful and open, without conceit or affectation of any kind – her manners just removed from the awkwardness and shyness of a girl; her person pleasing, and, when in good looks, pretty – and her mind about as ignorant and uninformed as the female mind at seventeen usually is (18).

Her complete lack of 'conceit or affectation' sets her apart from a number of this novel's other characters, and it reminds us how uncommon 'the common feelings of common life' can be. More than that, however, as the observant Henry notes, her artlessness is her strength:

> 'With you, it is not, How is such a one likely to be influenced? What is the inducement most likely to act upon such a person's feelings, age, situation, and probable habits of life considered? – but, how should *I* be influenced, what would be *my* inducement in acting so and so?' (132).

What Henry notices is not Catherine's inability to enter into another's situation, but her unawareness of less admirable human promptings; and an important part of this honesty to her own feelings is an innocent certainty of self.

In the conversation that takes place between Henry and Catherine after they have been introduced, the butt of his lively banter is how people in their situation usually talk and behave:

> 'Have you been long in Bath, madam?'
> 'About a week, sir,' replied Catherine, trying not to laugh.
> 'Really!' with affected astonishment.
> 'Why should you be surprized, sir?'

'Why, indeed!' said he, in his natural tone – 'but some emotion must appear to be raised by your reply, and surprize is more easily assumed, and not less reasonable than any other. – Now let us go on. Were you never here before, madam?'

'Never, sir.'

'Indeed! Have you yet honoured the Upper Rooms?'

'Yes, sir, I was there last Monday.'

'Have you been to the theatre?'

'Yes, sir, I was at the play on Tuesday.'

'To the concert?'

'Yes, sir, on Wednesday.'

'And are you altogether pleased with Bath?'

'Yes – I like it very well.'

'Now I must give one smirk, and then we may be rational again' (26).

An amused Catherine enters into the spirit of Henry's raillery, even though, because of her youth and ignorance, she feels less assured than her partner: 'Catherine turned away her head, not knowing whether she might venture to laugh.' Here she is only undecided about what her open response to him should be, for her actual response to what he says is neither negative nor undecided.

A more complex example of their mutual interest in each other occurs when Henry talks to Mrs Allen of Catherine's gown. He appears 'strange' (28) to her – though she leaves the word unsaid – when he expresses his fears that her gown will fray with washing. Henry is, of course, consciously humouring Mrs Allen: neither he nor Catherine is really caught up in such a world. That 'strange' which almost comes to her lips is, however, an indication that something between them has caught – that something unusual in Henry has indeed called 'forth her sensibility' (16). We cannot regret that she is not explicit because, however it might have furthered an equality based on a reciprocally stated recognition of each other, it would doubtless have weakened our sense of what is beginning to exist between them. Theirs is an unusual meeting that requires further and more subtle exploration, as though a precious quality in human relationships, almost an enticing privacy of which each is aware, could not be adequately reflected in early direct statement. Catherine seemingly recognises this for, pressed to tell Henry her thoughts, she refuses; and at this he makes a telling observation:

> 'Thank you; for now we shall soon be acquainted, as I am authorized to tease you on this subject whenever we meet, and nothing in the world advances intimacy so much' (29).

Such teasing was regarded by Jane Austen as a piquant form of sexual by-play,[1] and this episode allows us to suggest the relevance of this for the quality in Catherine that has so aroused Henry's interest. Just as she has noticed his strangeness, so he seems aware of some tenacity of self on her part, a resilience or strength or unusualness in her character he can only approach by probing at. What follows from this is a mutual interest and attentiveness, a special kind of recognition of each other, an intimacy between them in which privacy must not only be recognised but be capable, in some reciprocal way, of being shared.[2] In suggesting this, Jane Austen is, I believe, implicitly answering the sentimental novel's spurious expectation of extensive indulgence in private sensation. She herself has much more important feelings and moments to chart. Nor are these negated by her remarks on what might or might not have been Catherine's dreams that night. Her sly allusion to the novelist Richardson's view, that 'no young lady can be justified in falling in love before the gentleman's love is declared' (29–30), does not at all reflect on the heroine, who leaves Henry Tilney and goes to bed 'with a strong inclination for continuing the acquaintance'.

Isabella Thorpe, in her shallowness and vulgarity, is a rather crude foil to Catherine, who, young and impressionable, is eager for her affection and therefore somewhat flattered by her attention. Catherine is also influenced by her brother James, who is blind to Isabella's faults because of his regard for her. As he says to his sister, 'She is just the kind of young woman I could wish to see you attached to; she has so much good sense, and is so thoroughly unaffected and amiable' (50). Catherine as yet lacks Henry's discrimination or experience of the world, and shows, in all innocence, a capacity for being receptive and open to others. There is, nevertheless, a hint that she cannot quite share her brother's enthusiasm when she replies to him in these words: 'I never was so happy before; and now you are come it will be more delightful than ever'. (51).

The Thorpes are always narrowly preoccupied with their own concerns. Isabella, despite her protestations of friendship, is selfish of her own interests in deserting Catherine to go off with James, while John Thorpe intrudes himself into the group with all the marks of someone who tries to hide his insignificance from himself. Everything of his must be better than other people's, his horse, his gig, his wine. Catherine takes some time to work him out because her own parents, 'plain matter-of-fact people', 'were not in the habit . . . of telling lies to increase their importance' (65–6). Thorpe's self-centred 'effusions of endless conceit' make him a thoroughgoing bore, since he cannot forget himself long enough to have any genuine regard for others. His is not conversation but mere 'talk' because everything, even novel-reading, is reduced to the level of his own limited interests. He cannot forget himself long enough to have any disinterested regard for others.

Whereas Isabella displays 'decided pretension' or 'resolute stilishness', Catherine is characterised as possessing 'the real delicacy of a generous mind' (55). We have already noted her initial response to Henry, which may be sharply contrasted with Isabella's boasted prowess in handling men: 'They are very often amazingly impertinent if you do not treat them with spirit, and make them keep their distance' (42). The difference between these two young women is indicated by the difference between the kind of pertness Isabella goes in for and Catherine's ability to appreciate good-humoured by-play in the conversation of Henry, who, as W. D. Howells has said, 'can laugh at her so caressingly'.[3] Isabella's teasing is not designed to establish genuine intimacy; instead it is generally designed to proclaim someone else's interest in her. In the word Catherine applies to John Thorpe, it is 'self-assured' (48), whether of the kind used against Captain Hunt (40), or in Isabella's reported 'scolding' (56) of James. In her reference to 'teasing', there is, moreover, none of the engaging warmth that Henry had given the word:

> 'I tell you, Mr. Morland,' she cried, 'I would not do such a thing for all the world. How can you be so teasing; only conceive, my dear Catherine, what your brother wants me to do. He wants me to dance with him again, though I tell him that it is a most improper thing, and entirely against the rules. It would make us the talk of the place, if we were not to change partners' (57).

The appeal to a third party, as well as the wider circle of 'talk' that is anticipated, is a just reflection of Isabella's shallow understanding of what is involved. Henry, by contrast, had proposed teasing Catherine in recognition of how this would draw them together. What he recognises in her responsiveness is the opposite of Isabella's kind of self-assurance – the unaffected ingenuousness of a truly receptive mind, one not narrowly preoccupied with itself.

Catherine's innocent certainty of self, which Henry so much prizes, can also be contrasted with what is implied by Isabella's claim that she and James have 'exactly' the same 'tastes' and 'opinions'. 'There was not', she says, 'a single point in which we differed' (71). This seems to argue a vacuity of taste or mind or, if not precisely that, something less than a meeting of distinct minds; whereas when Catherine and Henry meet there is no loss of individual selfhood. Moreover, when Isabella supposes that if her friend had witnessed the complete coincidence of her and James's tastes and opinions she 'would have made some droll remark or other about it', an uncomprehending Catherine denies that she would. Such artlessness partly stems, as so often, from her innocence; but it also indicates her unwillingness to intrude on what does not concern her, as well as her sense of the inherent indelicacy of any such remark: 'Indeed you do me injustice; I would not have made so improper a remark upon any account; and besides, I am sure it would never have entered my head.'

Catherine, neither self-preoccupied nor self-defensive, seems in no need of irony as a protective defence against the world. This may explain why critics have alternatively viewed her as a 'goose' (though 'a very engaging goose') or as 'too simple and too slight . . . to assert the claim of personal feeling and value beyond mere function'.[4] Admittedly her artlessness can border on naïveté. When Henry, on hearing that in the country she can only 'go and call on Mrs. Allen', exclaims, 'What a picture of intellectual poverty', Catherine unwittingly applies this remark only to herself: 'Oh! yes. I shall never be in want of something to talk of again to Mrs. Allen, or any body else. I really believe I shall always be talking of Bath' (79). More endearingly naïve is Catherine's lack of disguise in making her feelings for Henry plain to his sister – though the Tilneys are not people to take advantage of such things.

Yet Catherine has an unerring sensitivity to certain basic values, and even though she is so lacking in an appreciation of the facetious, she proves her right to respond as she does by the depth of her own feelings. When Henry later suggests that Isabella 'is in love with James, and flirts with Frederick', Catherine immediately replies, 'Oh! no, not flirts. A woman in love with one man cannot flirt with another' (151). Nor is she disposed to accept Henry's witty attempt to prove that 'a country-dance' is 'an emblem of marriage' (76). Her 'fresh feelings of every sort' (79), which Henry so readily responds to, do not extend to her giving these things an equal weight in her mind:

> 'To be sure, as you state it, all this sounds very well; but
> still they are so very different. – I cannot look upon
> them at all in the same light, nor think the same duties
> belong to them' (77).

Henry had intended to guard against the further unwelcome intrusion of John Thorpe, but, as her partner, he has a better guarantee than any his analogy can give when Catherine declares that she does not *want* to talk' to anybody else (78). While there is no artifice in Catherine's reply, it disarmingly indicates her own interest in Henry.

Catherine's refreshing lack of sophistication also leads her to put the best possible construction on Captain Tilney's wish to dance with Isabella – so much so that Henry observes, 'How very little trouble it can give you to understand the motive of other people's actions' (132). Asked for his meaning, he replies,

> 'I only meant that your attributing my brother's wish of
> dancing with Miss Thorpe to good-nature alone,
> convinced me of your being superior in good-nature
> yourself to all the rest of the world' (133).

Good nature like hers encourages her to be entirely unaware of disingenuousness in human relationships.

Despite the evidence that is afforded her in the Pump-room,

> it seemed to her that Captain Tilney was falling in love with Isabella, and Isabella unconsciously encouraging him; unconsciously it must be, for Isabella's attachment to James was as certain and well acknowledged as her engagement. To doubt her truth or good intentions was impossible (148).

Catherine remains untouched by selfish or sophistical behaviour and it is 'the fine instinct which runs through her simplicity'[5] that gives *Northanger Abbey* its peculiar freshness.

The proposed excursion to Clifton leads to the engagement of Isabella and James, which in turn leads to John Thorpe's enigmatic wooing of Catherine. The behaviour of the Thorpes on these occasions furthers our sense of their self-centredness. In speaking to Catherine before he sets off for London, John accepts what he takes to be her implicit encouragement in a way that makes him seem unaware of anything beyond his own point of view. Though this brief episode is a neat piece of situational comedy, it catches him out in a lie when he protests that 'fortune is nothing' (124), and it ends by implying that he has no thought for anyone but himself: 'She hurried away, leaving him to the undivided consciousness of his own happy address, and her explicit encouragement.' 'Undivided consciousness' underlines the point we have already noticed, namely, that any process of sharing in such a situation is impossible. Isabella's self-centredness is even more obvious. At first she says, 'The very first day that Morland came to us last Christmas – the very first moment I beheld him – my heart was irrecoverably gone' (118); yet when she learns of the consent of the Morlands, her thoughts belie this earlier protestation. They reveal only her concern for personal and social aggrandisement:

She saw herself at the end of a few weeks, the gaze and admiration of every new acquaintance at Fullerton, the envy of every valued old friend in Putney, with a carriage at her command, a new name on her tickets, and a brilliant exhibition of hoop rings on her finger (122).

In contrast to this is what characterises the three young people in their walk around Beechen Cliff. A necessary basis for real conversation (as opposed to mere 'talk') is the kind of 'equal good will' with which Henry's sister Eleanor returns Catherine's 'advances' (72). This ensures that between them things can be 'spoken with simplicity and truth, and without personal conceit'. Not only do the often differing individual views of the three young people make for a genuine exchange of opinion, but their good-humoured responsiveness to one another furthers the sense of intimacy that exists among them. We are, of course, most interested in what flows between Catherine and Henry yet the presence of his sister is important for the sense it gives of a kind of surrogate relationship which allows Catherine to seem even closer to him. When he picks her up for an imprecise use of language, Eleanor suggestively remarks,

> 'Miss Morland, he is treating you exactly as he does his sister. He is for ever finding fault with me, for some incorrectness of language, and now he is taking the same liberty with you' (107–8).

Richard Simpson long ago pointed out that Jane Austen

> seems to be saturated with the Platonic idea that the giving and receiving of knowledge, the active formation of another's character, or the more passive growth under another's guidance, is the truest and strongest foundation of love.[6]

More recently, Lionel Trilling has argued that our author 'was committed to the ideal of "intelligent love", according to which the deepest and truest relationship that can exist between human beings is pedagogic'.[7] There is something pedagogic about Henry which Catherine's appealing ignorance is in a position to respond to, yet she too has something to offer in return. For Austen's heroines, education is not simply a matter of acquiring certain branches of knowledge, but of the refinement and expression of the individual intelligence. In this restructuring of contemporary notions of the self, there seems to be an anticipation of J. S. Mill's notion of individuality as something that grows and develops 'itself on all sides, according to the tendency of the inward forces which make it a living thing.'[8]

In Henry there is a tendency towards a certain self-dramatisation in respect of clarity and logic; and admittedly he does have to unravel the misunderstanding that arises over Catherine's remark that 'something very shocking indeed, will soon come out in London':

'Come, shall I make you understand each other, or leave you to puzzle out an explanation as you can? No – I will be noble. I will prove myself a man, no less by the generosity of my soul than the clearness of my head' (112).

Henry's comments on landscape and his 'lecture on the picturesque' (111) have, however, for Catherine the effect of contradicting 'the very few notions she had entertained on the matter before': 'It seemed as if a good view were no longer to be taken from the top of an high hill, and that a clear blue sky was no longer a proof of a fine day' (110). Though the irony here belongs to neither character, there is a hint of its being pointed rather more in Henry's direction.[9] Moreover, in their discussion of history, though Catherine's appears to be the wrong side of the

11

argument, there is a freshness about her comments that is directly informed by her own experience: 'I can read poetry and plays, and things of that sort, and do not dislike travels. But history, real solemn history, I cannot be interested in.' (108)

The implications of this exchange, and the Aristotelian stance Catherine unwittingly takes, extend beyond this episode and impinge on the Northanger section of the novel. We can note her youthful exuberance and credulity in allowing her expectation of reality to be shaped by the extravagant fantasies she has allowed to captivate her imagination; but we can also ask whether life is totally without a darker side or colouring. One problem with the Gothic section in this novel is the way it is textured. The style in which Catherine responds to the assumed Gothic paraphernalia is in contrast to the unbookish freshness with which, in other respects, she articulates her feelings; Marvin Mudrick has made the point that it 'demands too abrupt a transition from Catherine the matter-of-fact ingénue to Catherine the self-appointed Gothic heroine'.[10] Despite, however, the element of truth in this, it is arguably too simple a formulation, too little in touch both with her strength of character and with the complexity and intimacy of the relationship that we have seen to be developing between Catherine and Henry. Nor is the implied satire of this section of the novel all at Catherine's expense. Though Henry Tilney is constantly useful to her in pointing out her folly, events unfold in his very own home which cause us to reflect on what he takes to be his timely note of sweet reason.

During their drive to Northanger, Henry teases Catherine by giving free rein to his fancy in imagining 'all the horrors' (157) she would expect to encounter in a place as old as the abbey. Coach trips were often portentous events in eighteenth-century fiction, and Henry does all he can to terrify Catherine during their drive. Aware of her willingness to indulge 'a raised, restless, and frightened imagination over the pages of Udolpho' (51), he has a ready-made subject to exploit. Seemingly he takes delight in his own inventiveness, and with his keen sense of the ridiculous is conscious of the 'interest' (160) he so thoroughly arouses. Catherine for her part, though willing enough to be teased, is forced to deny being taken in by his narrative:

> Catherine, recollecting herself, grew ashamed of her eagerness, and began earnestly to assure him that her attention had been fixed without the smallest apprehension of really meeting with what he related.

Several times it is suggested that Catherine is somehow beside herself when she lets her fondness for the Gothic take hold of her imagination. Accordingly 'recollecting' in a passage such as this has something of its vestigial sense, as though the heroine needs to pull herself together. Though Jane Austen does not make the point so insistently as she will in her next novel, the importance of self-possession is implicitly touched on here. It is also obliquely hinted at, after Catherine has learnt the truth about Isabella, in Henry's question to her whether 'you feel . . . that, in losing Isabella, you lose half yourself' (207). Catherine 'after a few moments' reflection' can honestly answer 'No'. Despite her openness to Isabella, her sense of herself has never been impaired or threatened. Yet she is not past filling her daydreams with the kinds of images from her reading that are so dear to her:

> Her passion for ancient edifices was next in degree to her passion for Henry Tilney – and castles and abbies made usually the charm of those reveries which his image did not fill (141).

As she listens to 'the tempest' on her first night at Northanger, she assents in imagination to what she hears:

Yes, these were characteristic sounds; – they brought to her recollection a countless variety of dreadful situations and horrid scenes, which such buildings had witnessed, and such storms ushered in (166–7).

A vocabulary drawn from the terminology of literature is used to reinforce our sense of the willing confusion Catherine experiences in refusing to separate reality from her reading. For example, Eleanor's words about her mother's room convey 'pages of intelligence to Catherine' (186). And when the 'precious manuscript' turns out to be mostly a laundry list, though Catherine feels 'humbled to the dust' (173), she does not easily lay aside her folly. Rather she lets her fancy become more extravagant still, until her absurdity is finally brought home to her. Before this happens, however, she gives such a blindly circumstantial interpretation to the shreds of evidence she collects about the General as to imagine him as a real life counterpart to Mrs Radcliffe's Montoni (187).

Catherine's house of Gothic cards collapses when Henry forces on her distinctions that she had been unable or unwilling to make herself:

> 'Dear Miss Morland, consider the dreadful nature of the suspicions you have entertained. What have you been judging from? Remember the country and age in which we live. Remember that we are English, that we are Christians. Consult your own understanding, your own sense of the probable, your own observation of what is passing around you' (197).

Henry's words prompt 'tears of shame' (198), and Catherine comes to realise that 'it had been all a voluntary, self-created delusion' (199). She acknowledges that everything had been 'forced to bend to one purpose by a mind which, before she entered the Abbey, had been craving to be frightened':

She saw that the infatuation had been created, the mischief settled long before her quitting Bath, and it seemed as if the whole might be traced to the influence of that sort of reading which she had there indulged (200).

Indeed, what Catherine comes to realise gives authority to the particular provenance of Jane Austen's characteristic insights:

Charming as were all Mrs. Radcliffe's works, and charming even as were the works of all her imitators, it was not in them perhaps that human nature, at least in the midland counties of England, was to be looked for (200).

For Catherine herself 'the anxieties of common life' begin 'soon to succeed to the alarms of romance' (201), but common life, as our heroine comes to learn, can produce alarm of its own. General Tilney's cruelty is reserved not for his former wife but for Catherine herself, and he turns her unceremoniously out of doors because she has disappointed his expectations of wealth. Seemingly polished and courteous, he proves harsh and unforgiving even in small things, while later Catherine hears enough from Henry 'to feel, that in suspecting General Tilney of either murdering or shutting up his wife, she had scarcely sinned against his character, or magnified his cruelty' (247). Though he does not quite prove to be a Montoni, he nevertheless proves to be sufficiently a monster in being so basely motivated by greed.

It is therefore too simplistic to conclude that Gothic fiction is satirised in *Northanger Abbey* through the figure of Catherine as its credulous devotee. Catherine comes to experience a greater distress than any she had fabricated for herself:

That room, in which her disturbed imagination had tormented her on her first arrival, was again the scene of agitated spirits and unquiet slumbers. Yet how different now the source of her inquietude from what it had been then – how mournfully superior in reality and substance (227).

Though the enormity of what happens to Catherine should not be exaggerated, the General's behaviour towards her effectively gives the lie to Henry's remarks about the sane and even tenor of English life. Even domestic life can be disturbing, its seemingly ordinary aspects masking an insidious ugliness. And it is in this realisation that the reader of *Northanger Abbey* is inevitably involved. An extravagant fiction that seems altogether too remote from the concerns of real life is replaced by our recognition of the pain and distress real life can give rise to.[11]

General Tilney's opposition to Henry's marrying Catherine is ultimately removed by the specious contrivance of having Eleanor marry a rich viscount. Jane Austen is here unable to meet the demands of her fiction except by 'fiction' of a spurious kind, and something of the amused exuberance of the earlier writer of burlesque persists in the way she draws self-conscious attention to her creaking machinery:

I have only to add – (aware that the rules of composition forbid the introduction of a character not connected with my fable) – that this was the very gentleman whose negligent servant left behind him that collection of washing-bills, resulting from a long visit at Northanger, by which my heroine was involved in one of her most alarming adventures (251).

But the interest of the novel transcends such things as these. Henry must come to claim Catherine because of what has developed between them.

Something of Henry's 'strangeness' can be seen in his words to his sister on being told that his brother Frederick might have become engaged to Isabella:

> 'Prepare for your sister-in-law, Eleanor, and such a
> sister-in-law as you must delight in! – Open, candid,
> artless, guileless, with affections strong but simple,
> forming no pretensions, and knowing no disguise'
> (206).

This (as Eleanor realises) is a picture not of Isabella but of Catherine, and Henry's words indicate the drift of his thoughts. In one sense they suggest his incredulity at the reported engagement, but in another and more important sense they declare his intentions towards Catherine. It is said that 'a persuasion of her partiality for him had been the only cause of giving her a serious thought' (243), but this explanation leaves too baldly out of account what has caught and held his attention. After she has been half-inclined to excuse Isabella's involvement with Captain Tilney, Henry says to Catherine:

> 'If you would stand by *your's* [i.e. your brother], you
> would not be much distressed by the disappointment of
> Miss Thorpe. But your mind is warped by an innate
> principle of general integrity, and therefore not access-
> ible to the cool reasonings of family partiality, or a
> desire of revenge' (219).

'Warped' reveals something of the defensiveness Henry feels on his brother's behalf; yet the context also indicates how exceptional he finds Catherine.

Her understanding admittedly benefits from knowing Henry, since there is much that he can teach her. She is also conscious of his 'astonishing generosity and nobleness of conduct' (201) in not betraying to anyone else her wild imaginings about his father. Yet what is bestowed is by no means one-sided. Catherine's 'fresh feelings of every sort' clearly captivate Henry, and in the encouragement he gives her he explicitly acknowledges what it is that so holds his attention. When, asked about her feelings on learning of Isabella's break with James, she admits to not feeling 'so very, very much afflicted as one would have thought', Henry responds by saying, 'You feel, as you always do, what is most to the credit of human nature. – Such feelings ought to be investigated, that they may know themselves' (207). Though, before this, Henry has been incipiently teasing Catherine (by imagining, for example, how she would not now 'go to a ball for the world'), his subsequent words reveal his appreciation of the kind of self-awareness she inherently possesses. Having a tendency to be extroverted himself, he comes to respect and even to need the kind of assurance that her individuality implies.[12] When at the ball she had told him that she did not '*want* to talk' to anybody else, Henry had significantly replied, 'Now you have given me a security worth having' (78).

Whereas Catherine feels grateful for his attention, Henry for his part feels grateful that she feels this for him. Yet gratitude is insufficient to describe what flows between them, unless we understand this in words borrowed from Milton:

> a grateful mind
> By owing owes not, but still pays, at once
> Indebted and discharged.[13]

Such reciprocity, or the intimacy that develops between them, has its origin in what has been present from their very first meeting, namely an intense interest in each other. To describe this as almost tactile would in one sense be going too far, yet it does have an element of that about it, of something immediate that catches and holds between them.

Elinor Dashwood

Sense and Sensibility has usually been written off as an inferior work. It has seemed too doctrinaire or didactic in following 'the format of the contrast-novel', with the result that its major figures have appeared (as they long ago did to Reginald Farrer) 'rather incarnate qualities than qualitied incarnations'.[1] Adverse views of Elinor Dashwood have ranged from 'good and nice' but 'only intermittently interesting', 'an aggregation of good qualities' but 'not a living person', to, on the less pleasant side, a character of 'boring causticity'.[2] By contrast her sister Marianne, though not seen as faultless, has seemed to possess a depth of feeling which Elinor knows nothing of.[3] Such criticism cannot be answered by quoting the initial description of Elinor, though what is said of her should not go unnoticed: 'She had an excellent heart; – her disposition was affectionate, and her feelings were strong' (6). One must also probe Elinor's presentation as a character, and this may well prove her to be more interesting than has generally been thought. Contrary to the usual view of either her stiffness or her fleeting presence in the novel, she is, I believe, not only flexible in responding to much more than merely conventional forms, but represents a moral centre of feeling and action that gives a constant focus to the events that surround her.

Elinor's responsiveness enables her both to be discriminating towards others and to have the related capacity of entering into what others besides herself are feeling. She has a deep sympathy for Marianne, though she believes her sister to act unwisely towards the dashing but dissembling Willoughby. And towards Edward Ferrars, who is, she learns, secretly engaged to Lucy Steele, she is able to respond without compromising either him or herself. While she feels the hurt of this situation, she does not allow it to blight what can only be friendship – until an unexpected turn of events allows them to share the kind of intimacy, as lovers, which has long been potentially theirs.

Elinor is most revealing of herself in the way she relates to Edward. During his absence from Barton Cottage, Marianne complains that her sister's 'self-command is invariable': 'When is she dejected or melancholy? When does she try to avoid society, or appear restless and dissatisfied in it?' (39). Moreover, when Edward, without explanation or apology, later takes his leave of Mrs Dashwood in a ' desponding' (104) frame of mind, Elinor seems resolved to go about her business without showing any undue emotion. Here, as on so many occasions, she shows that she can 'exert herself' (7); but Marianne, who always indulges her own emotions, finds Elinor's conduct hard to accept:

> Such behaviour as this, so exactly the reverse of her own, appeared no more meritorious to Marianne, than her own had seemed faulty to her. The business of self-command she settled very easily; – with strong affections it was impossible, with calm ones it could have no merit. That her sister's affections *were* calm, she dared not deny, though she blushed to acknowledge it; and of the strength of her own, she gave a very striking proof, by still loving and respecting that sister, in spite of this mortifying conviction (104).

This implied magnanimity works, however, against Marianne. It is Elinor who has controlled her feelings to spare 'her mother and sisters . . . much solicitude on her account', and Marianne, whose devotion to Willoughby is such as to put herself at risk, has no reason to boast the contrast with herself. For her 'the business of self-command' is a merely negative quality: no 'merit' attaches to it when it is practised by someone with tepid feelings, while for someone 'with strong affections' like herself it is purely an irrelevance.

Elinor's early long speech on Edward's 'sense' and 'goodness' is, admittedly, unconvincing (20). It is not just that her sentiments have to be inferred from such 'unreserved conversation' between Edward and herself as neither Marianne nor the reader has witnessed; it is also that her sentiments are expressed so formally: 'His mind is well-informed, his enjoyment of books exceedingly great, his imagination lively, his observation just and correct, and his taste delicate and pure.' It is one thing for Elinor to endorse such attributes, but quite another for them to be presented in this way. Marianne's 'I shall very soon think him handsome, Elinor, if I do not now' awakens Elinor to a livelier response. Though she seeks to modify the conclusion her sister has inevitably drawn, her attempt to do so merely suggests how deep her interest in Edward is, and she is prompted to give a more cautious yet somehow more intimate account of her hopes and feelings.

When Elinor implies her 'esteem' for Edward, her mother says that she herself has never 'known what it was to separate esteem and love' (16). Later, when Elinor suffers under the 'heavy blow' of learning of Edward's secret engagement, she can remain conscious that he has 'done nothing to forfeit her esteem' (141). Such a recognition involves her having a clear sense of Edward and what is attractive about him as something that is, so to speak, distinct from her sense of herself. This is necessary to provide the basis for a deeper relationship that, given

other, more favourable circumstances, can develop between them.

When Elinor first learns of Edward's secret engagement,
her 'indignation' makes her feel 'for a short time . . . only
for herself' (139). But 'other considerations' soon arise,
and her ability to feel beyond herself enables her to weep
for him 'more than for herself' (140). She notes 'his
integrity, his delicacy, and well-informed mind', which
could never be happy with Lucy Steele as a wife. Elinor
sees in Lucy's behaviour at Barton Park 'the thorough
want of delicacy, of rectitude, and integrity of mind' (127),
while Lucy's 'insincerity' (150) and 'self-interest' (151)
become obvious in their conversations about Edward.
Even though Elinor is unable to 'deny herself the comfort
of endeavouring to convince Lucy that her heart was
unwounded' (142), she soon realises the danger of being
drawn into such a conversation: 'Elinor thought it wisest
to make no answer to this, lest they might provoke each
other to an unsuitable increase of ease and unreserve' (150).
Obviously no real intimacy can exist between these two
young women, who have nothing of a reciprocal nature
they can share. In fact Elinor is conscious that she is, in a
sense, merely playing into Lucy's hands: 'She felt such
conversations to be an indulgence which Lucy did not
deserve, and which were dangerous to herself' (151).
When Lucy later arrives in London her impertinence
knows no bounds, and Elinor is obliged to exercise all her
self-restraint in order to prevent herself from adding to
Lucy's sense of triumph: 'Elinor perfectly understood her,
and was forced to use all her self-command to make it
appear that she did *not*' (217–18).

Admittedly Elinor feels, as she journeys towards
London, 'how blank was her own prospect, how cheerless
her own state of mind' (159) by comparison with the
happiness that might await Marianne. Yet she responds to
this almost immediately by resolving to open her sister's

eyes if Willoughby should seem indifferent, or, 'should it be otherwise', by schooling herself 'to avoid every selfish comparison, and banish every regret which might lessen her satisfaction in the happiness of Marianne'. Such self-command is more positive than stoical, more courageous than negative, because it leads to a response in which the self is engaged. The confidence Lucy imparts also calls for inner reserves. Elinor is forced to 'command herself enough to guard every suspicion of the truth from her mother and sisters' (141). She rightly realises that she is 'stronger alone'. The secret she is forced to keep, though initially so surprising and painful, and though virtually extinguishing all hope for the future, enables her to come to a better understanding of Edward's behaviour in relation to herself. She refuses to let it blight her life, and instead directs her feeling outwards, towards Edward himself, thereby ensuring a regard that preserves, at the very least, a high level of personal esteem. Their parting before his presumed marriage to Lucy is managed

> with a very earnest assurance on *her* side of her
> unceasing good wishes for his happiness in every change
> of situation that might befal him; on *his*, with rather an
> attempt to return the same good will, than the power of
> expressing it (290).

There is an opportunity of contrasting Elinor's behaviour with her sister's when Willoughby enters the story and literally sweeps Marianne off her feet: 'His person and air were equal to what her fancy had ever drawn for the hero of a favourite story' (43). Marianne is so completely unreserved with Willoughby, seeking such an immediate coincidence of their tastes and opinions, that Elinor tries to warn her of the fact that a true and lasting intimacy cannot be promoted by these means:

> 'Well, Marianne,' said Elinor, as soon as he had left
> them, 'for *one* morning I think you have done pretty

well. You have already ascertained Mr. Willoughby's opinion in almost every matter of importance. . . . But how is your acquaintance to be long supported, under such extraordinary dispatch of every subject for discourse?' (47)

This incisive pleasantry is, however, misrepresented by Marianne's self-defensiveness:

'I see what you mean. I have been too much at my ease, too happy, too frank. I have erred against every common-place notion of decorum; I have been open and sincere where I ought to have been reserved, spiritless, dull, and deceitful.' (47–48).

But Elinor is not advocating that her sister be 'spiritless, dull, and deceitful'; nor do these epithets apply to her own behaviour. Certainly she encourages Marianne to be more 'reserved', or less unreserved; yet this, after all, can have its positive side.

Reserve ensures that the privacy of others is not violated – something Willoughby is guilty of in his uncalled-for remarks on Colonel Brandon. The difference between his calculated slur and Marianne's ready agreement is that Willoughby, in his antitheses and generalisations, refuses to commit himself personally, except by implication, whereas Marianne at least has the honesty to do so in an undisguised, outright way. Yet, as the action of the novel makes plain, reserve is not merely important in preventing an unfair or premature judgment of others and therefore in allowing them their due; it is also important in ensuring one's own privacy, which Marianne, because she is careless about it, is in real danger of losing. Elinor is not advocating that her sister behave like Lady Middleton, whose 'reserve was a mere calmness of manner with which sense had nothing to do', for her ladyship is 'towards her husband and her mother . . . the same as to them', and 'intimacy' with her is 'therefore neither to be looked for nor desired' (55). Elinor realises that intimacy can only result from a privacy capable of being shared, and it is privacy of this sort that the singular (rather than private) behaviour of Marianne precludes. At certain points we are, indeed, sympathetically aware of the false conception Marianne has of such intimacy. In a later letter to Willoughby she says that their 'intimacy at Barton' (187) had led her to expect something very different from his present behaviour towards her. Much earlier, in answer to Elinor's caution that Willoughby is 'a man so little, or at least so lately known' (58), Marianne gives her opinion of what constitutes intimacy. With telling dramatic irony she says:

> 'I am much better acquainted with him, than I am with any other creature in the world, except yourself and mama. It is not time or opportunity that is to determine intimacy; – it is disposition alone' (59).

Marianne fails to include herself among those she knows well. She does not seek to possess herself but Willoughby; and there is ironic pathos in her confidence of having so 'thoroughly possessed' his 'whole heart' (141). In her youthfulness she is unable to entertain the idea of a lover whose sensibility does not duplicate or provide a mirror-image of her own, and what she therefore fails to understand is the perception expressed by a recent poet that 'the joy of being two' involves

> Not seeking to annihilate
> Distinction, as self-lovers do.[4]

The exclusiveness of Marianne's kind of self-absorption is no basis for intimacy, and Willoughby exploits this trait in Marianne by talking to her 'only of herself' (190). There is, then, a selfishness (however differently motivated) on both sides, and it is only when Elinor mentions

Willoughby as 'selfish' (351) that Marianne suddenly and painfully recognises her own former 'folly' (352).

By forfeiting her privacy in being so 'unreserved' (81), Marianne makes herself singularly vulnerable. She leaves herself 'exposed . . . to some very impertinent remarks' (68); as she later admits, 'Perhaps, Elinor, it *was* rather ill-judged in me to go to Allenham' (69). But it is not just Mrs Jennings's teasing that is to her a source of 'great confusion' (67). Later in London, because she writes to Willoughby, and Mrs Jennings and her daughter talk of her engagement as a settled thing, Marianne has to suffer having it known that he is engaged to another. True, she seeks, in the manner of a tragic heroine, to put a bold front on her wretchedness: 'Misery such as mine has no pride. I care not who knows that I am wretched. The triumph of seeing me so may be open to all the world' (189). Nevertheless her wish to return home shows some part of what she is suffering:

> 'I cannot stay here long, I cannot stay to endure the questions and remarks of all these people. The Middletons and Palmers – how am I to bear their pity? The pity of such a woman as Lady Middleton!' (191)

It is this kind of thing which Elinor, by suggesting 'the propriety of some self-command' (53), would seek to guard against. The degree of distress that would otherwise be hers is clear from the scene in which Mrs Jennings quizzes the youngest sister about 'Elinor's particular favourite':

> 'I must not tell, may I, Elinor?'
> This of course made every body laugh; and Elinor tried to laugh too. But the effort was painful. She was convinced that Margaret had fixed on a person, whose name she could not bear with composure to become a standing joke with Mrs Jennings.
> Marianne felt for her most sincerely (61).

Elinor is forced to endure the threat of something becoming public that she would wish to keep private, and she is constrained to do this within a social context that places its own demands on her. Lady Middleton, however, interposes only because of her 'great dislike of all such inelegant subjects of raillery as delighted her husband and mother' (62); while Colonel Brandon, who always shows a 'genuine attention to other people' (338), aids Lady Middleton in turning the subject for another and better reason, because he is 'on every occasion mindful of the feelings of others' (62). His sense of propriety includes an innate delicacy in realising that certain things should remain private and therefore not be subject to the prying eyes of others.

When Edward appears at Barton Cottage he has a painful secret to keep. His natural shyness is therefore overlaid by a distance in his manner which ensures that he does not give himself away. Even Elinor is 'vexed and half angry' (89) with him: 'His coldness and reserve mortified her severely.' Marianne calls him reserved to his face:

> Edward started – 'Reserved! Am I reserved, Marianne?'
> 'Yes, very.'
> 'I do not understand you,' replied he, colouring. 'Reserved! – how, in what manner? What am I to tell you? What can you suppose?'
> Elinor looked surprised at his emotion, but trying to laugh off the subject, she said to him, 'Do not you know my sister well enough to understand what she means? Do not you know that she calls every one reserved who does not talk as fast, and admire what she admires as rapturously as herself?' (94–5)

Despite this, Elinor notices 'with great uneasiness' Edward's 'reservedness of . . . manner towards her', which 'contradicted one moment what a more animated look had intimated the preceding one' (96). Characteristically she has

27

to exert herself in order to preserve her equanimity and keep the conversation going – whereas Marianne's devotion to sensibility is rather prescriptive in that she never wonders or asks herself what might lie behind Edward's manner.

Elinor is conscious of this trait in Marianne as something that goes deeper than Edward's more superficial view of the younger sister. She realises that Marianne's 'gaiety' is neither as disinterested nor as self-fulfilling as it might seem: 'I should hardly call her a lively girl – she is very earnest, very eager in all she does – sometimes talks a great deal and always with animation – but she is not often really merry' (93). Marianne tries to counter this by supposing it has always been Elinor's 'doctrine' to make 'our judgments . . . subservient to those of our neighbours'. Elinor, however, sets her right by stressing that one needs to behave flexibly and yet remain true to one's inner lights in coping with the demands of a particular situation:

> 'My doctrine has never aimed at the subjection of the understanding. All I have ever attempted to influence has been the behaviour. You must not confound my meaning. I am guilty, I confess, of having often wished you to treat our acquaintance in general with greater attention; but when have I advised you to adopt their sentiments or conform to their judgment in serious matters?' (94)

It has been said that 'behaviour and understanding are not so easily separated' – that 'in a novel one must judge characters by their behaviour . . . because finally there is nothing else'.[5] But this confuses the different meanings that 'behaviour' has in each context, for the behaviour of a character in a novel comprises all that the reader sees – thoughts and inner feelings and principles as well as behaviour towards others in a particular context. Elinor is suggesting what should be preserved intact within the self – what must neither be dissipated by the claims of others, nor self-centredly refuse to admit that such claims can exist. More than that, this episode illustrates how Elinor's witty yet considerate plain-speaking can flourish in a situation that encourages genuine intimacy – in the company of those she knows well, like Edward and her immediate family.

Something of Elinor's animation rubs off on Edward's manner. When he talks to Marianne on the subject of 'taste' (97), he concludes by saying, 'I have more pleasure in a snug farm-house than a watch-tower – and a troop of tidy, happy villagers please me better than the finest banditti in the world' (98). This is successful baiting, as Marianne's horrified reaction proves. Yet his other attempt at witty good humour misfires on him. Hearing of Willoughby, and inferring from Marianne's earlier remark about hunters the reason for it, he says to her 'in a whisper', 'I guess that Mr. Willoughby hunts' (100). The 'earnestness and warmth' which greet his remark are enough to disconcert him, 'for had he not imagined it to be a joke for the good of her acquaintance in general, founded only on a something or a nothing between Mr. Willoughby and herself, he would not have ventured to mention it.' Exchanges such as this indicate the subtlety with which Jane Austen can adumbrate character and values. Edward has broken through his innate reserve from the best motive, only to find that he has trespassed on something which should have remained private. Though Marianne is not offended, indeed rather the reverse, this does not excuse to him the otherwise innocent liberty he has taken.

Edward's delicacy on this occasion follows on the embarrassment Marianne has caused him in commenting on a lock of hair in his ring. Paradoxically it is her kind of unreserve which, often so unthinking, can lead her to be inattentive to the claims of others. When the two sisters journey to London with Mrs Jennings, Marianne remains self-absorbed, 'wrapt in her own meditations' (160), leaving to Elinor the task of responding to the older woman:

> To atone for this conduct . . . Elinor took immediate possession of the post of civility which she had assigned herself, behaved with the greatest attention to Mrs. Jennings, talked with her, laughed with her, and listened to her whenever she could; and Mrs. Jennings on her side treated them *both* with all possible kindness. (my italics)

Elinor always honours her social responsibility, however much it might sometimes cost her to be properly attentive. Later, we see the importance of the effort she makes, for Mrs Jennings proves in the end to be a friend to both sisters.

Inimical to Elinor's self-possession is not only Marianne's self-absorption but her irritability, a trait that is mentioned more than once.[6] What it suggests is a fretting within the self, a self-defensive tightening against admitting outside claims and therefore a radical inability to engage in the creative give-and-take of personal relationships. When Elinor is obliged to enlighten her sister about her own situation, Marianne confesses how unthinkingly self-centred her own behaviour has been:

> 'Oh! Elinor,' she cried, 'you have made me hate myself for ever. – How barbarous have I been to you! – you, who have been my only comfort, who have borne with me in all my misery, who have seemed to be only suffering for me' (264).

On recovering from her grave illness, which has given her 'leisure and calmness for serious recollection' (345),

Marianne is able to acknowledge 'all the fretful selfishness' (346) of her past behaviour:

> 'Every body seemed injured by me. The kindness, the unceasing kindness of Mrs. Jennings, I had repaid with ungrateful contempt. To the Middletons, the Palmers, the Steeles, to every common acquaintance even, I had been insolent and unjust; with an heart hardened against their merits, and a temper irritated by their very attention.'

When Marianne has begun to be self-critical, she can practise her promised discretion even in the face of allusions to Edward and Lucy which would earlier have thrown her into a paroxysm of emotion: 'Such advances towards heroism in her sister, made Elinor feel equal to any thing herself' (265). Despite the surrounding irony, a page is here turned on the earlier sentimental heroine in favour of a less demonstrative heroism, one that proves, like Elinor's, to be more thoroughly grounded in an intelligent and unassuming appraisal of what it suffers or needs to cope with. While the dialectical structure of *Sense and Sensibility* is foreshadowed in its title, what really holds it together is Elinor's awareness of herself and others. Her presence permeates the novel, and the interest of her situation is heightened by our sense of events that are so effectively stacked against her. If, however, the novel were merely made up of these, it would have little interest beyond the creation of prolonged suspense followed by its release. What we have in addition is matter of solid substance, a moral centre of feeling and action that encompasses far more than temporary loss or seeming isolation.

Because Marianne has generally lacked Elinor's discrimination, she has wilfully refused to see Willoughby as somehow independent of herself. As he says in his final interview with Elinor, when trying to account for his earlier behaviour towards her sister, 'I endeavoured, by every means in my power, to make myself pleasing to her, without any design of returning her affection' (320). Marianne has from the beginning tended in imagination to create Willoughby what she would have him, and 'if any difference appeared, any objection arose, it lasted no longer than till the force of her arguments and the brightness of her eyes could be displayed' (47). But Elinor knows that knowledge of another cannot be so easily or spuriously gained. Rather it must begin in uncertainties or mistakes that can only be progressively resolved. When Edward seemingly accepts her view that he has been mistaken in thinking Marianne gay and lively, Elinor indicates how difficult it can be to come to a proper judgment of someone:

> 'I have frequently detected myself in such kind of mistakes . . . in a total misapprehension of character in some point or other: fancying people so much more gay or grave, or ingenious or stupid than they really are, and I can hardly tell why, or in what the deception originated. Sometimes one is guided by what they say of themselves, and very frequently by what other people say of them, without giving oneself time to deliberate and judge' (93).

Such a passage prompts us to question too restrictive an interpretation of Elinor's moral sense. Though critics respond to Marianne's obvious vitality, her recourse to the demands of 'strong affections' is not endorsed in the novel; nor would Jane Austen, as a recognisable descendant of Dr Johnson, have felt a kinship with her apparent espousal of a Shaftesburian morality. Elinor, in a passage like the above, surely appears more flexible than Mudrick's description of her as the embodiment of 'the formal conscience'. And given this assessment of her (by contrast with her younger sister), it is hardly surprising the same critic suggests that in her interview with Willoughby we can see 'Elinor – and presumably the author – almost in love, and quite amorally in love, with him'.[7] Elinor's insistence on 'time to deliberate and judge' shows she is herself wary about snap decisions, however strong immediate impressions might be; and this attitude of hers seems more genuinely responsive (and even more generous) than Marianne's often is. Elinor is moved, for example, by Willoughby's manner and appearance, as well as by the confessed ardour of his love for her sister, and she thinks of him 'rather in proportion, as she soon acknowledged within herself – to his wishes than to his merits' (333). 'Reflection' (349), however, enables her to put all she has experienced and heard into a more objective perspective:

> 'The whole of his behaviour . . . has been grounded on selfishness. . . . His own enjoyment, or his own ease, was, in every particular, his ruling principle. . . . He regrets what he has done. And why does he regret it? – Because he finds it has not answered to himself' (351).

This is Elinor talking to the recovered Marianne, and therefore avoiding any 'embellishment of tenderness to lead the fancy astray' (349). She will, however, always 'feel a pang for Willoughby' (339), as the reader will too. Yet it is ultimately difficult to discount Elinor's conclusion; and it is precisely such objectivity which needs 'time' to establish itself.

Mature deliberation is not, of course, characteristic of Willoughby or Marianne. 'In hastily forming and giving his opinion of other people' Willoughby displays 'a want of caution which Elinor could not approve' (49). Such 'caution' implies rather more than Mudrick assumes when he glosses Willoughby and Marianne as 'young and incautiously, thoughtlessly – though deeply – in love'.[8] What both these characters have finally to learn is that incautious unreserve can lead to the loss of real happiness through unwise or incomplete personal commitment, whereas Elinor's remark suggests that without mature deliberation as an indispensable part of the moral process people will be led to behave unfairly to both others and themselves. Mudrick nevertheless seems right in suggesting that there is something of the 'missionary forgiving spirit'[9] in Marianne's recantation. In so thoroughly blaming herself, she exalts the Middletons and Palmers as virtual paragons. Elinor's response is always more balanced, and in being this it allows for her attitude to grow or change (as the reader's does towards Mrs Jennings) without denying or contradicting itself by embracing extremes.

Perhaps this has tended to be obscured for critics because of the caution Elinor counsels and displays throughout a novel that is so noticeably filled with secrets.[10] In such a world, caution becomes necessary if one is not going to be placed in an impossible position (as Marianne is in London and as Elinor might have been if she had divulged Lucy and Edward's secret). Her self-possession can be opposed to what Mrs Dashwood later calls Marianne's 'prepossession for that worthless young man' (337). Marianne's 'prepossession', her eager espousal (or rejection) of people and things is ultimately prejudicial to the kind of discretion that self-possession implies. It allows no room for an intimacy to develop that is based on mutual sharing.

Not merely Elinor's intelligence but the sensitivity of her depth of feeling is implied in her self-possession. While her mother trusts to her daughter's 'temperate account of her own disappointment' (335), Mrs Dashwood, on being told of the marriage of 'Mr. Ferrars', is nevertheless 'shocked to perceive by Elinor's countenance how much she really suffered' (353). Elinor does not wear her heart on her sleeve; yet the strength of her feelings can be inferred from the self-restraint she needs to exercise in order to control them. Edward, too, has the capacity to be deeply moved, and perhaps the clearest indication of this occurs after he has announced to Elinor news of his brother's marriage to Lucy:

> He rose from his seat and walked to the window, apparently from not knowing what to do; took up a pair of scissars that lay there, and while spoiling both them and their sheath by cutting the latter to pieces as he spoke, said, in an hurried voice . . . (360)

Elinor's acceptance of Edward, after his release from his unfortunate engagement, results 'in such a genuine, flowing, grateful cheerfulness, as his friends had never witnessed in him before' (362). Elinor, too, finds her happiness almost too much to bear: 'She was everything by turns but tranquil. . . . It required several hours to give sedateness to her spirits, or any degree of tranquillity to her heart' (363). In her later novels Jane Austen comes to manage better such moments as this, though we are, even so, left here in no doubt of the 'happiness' (380) Elinor will enjoy during her marriage to Edward. Our confidence of this arises, in part, from the personal qualities of each, but it arises also from our sense of what they will genuinely share. The strongest intimation of this occurs in a passage which reminds us of what Elinor herself had said about Marianne's seemingly exhaustive conversations with Willoughby, but which indicates, more importantly, how differently Elinor and Edward will express themselves towards each other:

> Though a very few hours spent in the hard labour of incessant talking will dispatch more subjects than can really be in common between any two rational creatures, yet with lovers it is different. Between *them* no subject is finished, no communication is even made, till it has been made at least twenty times over (363–4).

Elizabeth Bennet

Pride and Prejudice contains the most famous opening sentence in English literature: 'It is a truth universally acknowledged, that a single man in possession of a good fortune, must be in want of a wife' (3). At the same time, no two characters would, on the face of it, seem less likely to marry than Elizabeth Bennet and Fitzwilliam Darcy. Because of his manner of slighting her at the ball, she has from the start 'no very cordial feelings towards him' (12); and so overwhelming is her initial 'prejudice' because of his seemingly repulsive 'pride', that the reader wonders by what process they could ever come together. Yet they do almost immediately notice each other; and that he can afterwards bring himself to propose to her indicates that something important has been passing between them – something sufficient, in itself, to begin to humanise Darcy.

Elizabeth's reaction to his initial rebuff is to tell the story 'with great spirit among her friends; for she had a lively, playful disposition, which delighted in any thing ridiculous' (12). It is his disdain which at first encourages her to exert herself against him. She says to Charlotte, 'He has a very satirical eye, and if I do not begin by being impertinent myself, I shall soon grow afraid of him' (24). Even Mr Collins notices her 'wit and vivacity' (106), qualities which he, however, expects will be duly tempered by 'the silence and respect' due to his patroness Lady

Catherine de Bourgh. But Elizabeth does not permit herself to feel inferior to Lady Catherine or her nephew. By giving free rein to her lively intelligence, she forces Darcy to converse with her as an equal.

Though he at first observes her critically, noticing that she has 'hardly a good feature in her face', he soon finds it 'rendered uncommonly intelligent by the beautiful expression of her dark eyes' and is 'caught' by the 'easy playfulness' of her 'manners' (23). While these are 'not those of the fashionable world', Darcy is bound to redefine the conventional view of female 'accomplishments' by what so interests him in Elizabeth. When her friend Charlotte Lucas insists that she 'play and sing' (24) to the assembled company, it is not Elizabeth's 'performance' (25) that captivates Darcy; instead it is the liveliness with which she seeks to confirm his dislike. She has mentioned to Charlotte why she has to exert herself against him, and soon has the opportunity of suiting her action to her words. On Darcy's approaching them 'though without seeming to have any intention of speaking', Elizabeth is provoked to address him:

> 'Did not you think, Mr. Darcy, that I expressed myself uncommonly well just now, when I was teazing Colonel Forster to give us a ball at Meryton?'
> 'With great energy; – but it is a subject which always makes a lady energetic.'
> 'You are severe on us.'
> 'It will be *her* turn soon to be teazed,' said Miss Lucas. 'I am going to open the instrument, Eliza, and you know what follows' (24).

The 'teasing' here works against Elizabeth not Darcy: Charlotte presses her to play, and Elizabeth's verbal display merely gives him the opportunity of turning her words to her seeming disadvantage. In future conversations, however, she does not so easily lose the advantage. Indeed, as she makes Darcy's words and manner the target of her wit, she forces him to modify both his own preconceptions and the air of aloof superiority he has too easily arrogated to himself. Her teasing of him becomes, in fact, the essence of her own 'performance' and the means of interesting him so thoroughly instead of (as she supposes) driving him away.

This becomes obvious during Elizabeth's first evening at Netherfield, when Miss Bingley seeks to ingratiate herself with Darcy by praising his sister Georgiana. There is, however, nothing in Miss Bingley's manner to animate Darcy, who comments as follows on the conventional list of female accomplishments mentioned by her brother:

> 'Your list of the common extent of accomplishments,' said Darcy, 'has too much truth. The word is applied to many a woman who deserves it no otherwise than by netting a purse, or covering a skreen. But I am very far from agreeing with you in your estimation of ladies in general. I cannot boast of knowing more than half a dozen, in the whole range of my acquaintance, that are really accomplished.'
> 'Nor I, I am sure,' said Miss Bingley.

Yet Darcy's proves an extreme view, extreme because apparently unrealistic, and Elizabeth is prompted to tackle him about it:

> 'Then,' observed Elizabeth, 'you must comprehend a great deal in your idea of an accomplished woman.'
> 'Yes; I do comprehend a great deal in it.'
> 'Oh! certainly,' cried his faithful assistant, 'no one can be really esteemed accomplished, who does not greatly surpass what is usually met with. A woman must have a thorough knowledge of music, singing, drawing, dancing, and the modern languages, to deserve the word; and besides all this, she must possess a certain something in her air and manner of walking, the tone of her voice,

her address and expressions, or the word will be but half deserved.'

'All this she must possess,' added Darcy, 'and to all this she must yet add something more substantial, in the improvement of her mind by extensive reading.'

'I am no longer surprised at your knowing *only* six accomplished women. I rather wonder now at your knowing *any*.'

'Are you so severe upon your own sex, as to doubt the possibility of all this?'

'*I* never saw such a woman. *I* never saw such capacity, and taste, and application, and elegance, as you describe, united' (39–40).

Bingley and his sister are replaced by Darcy and Elizabeth, who come to have the conversation between them. Each closely engages with the other's words despite the polite framework of social converse. Miss Bingley only ventures a cutting remark when Elizabeth has left the room, but receives no comfort from the irony Darcy employs in turning her observation back upon herself. True, both she and her sister cry out against 'the injustice' (40) of Elizabeth's 'implied doubt', and protest that they know 'many' who answer to Darcy's description of an accomplished woman; but theirs is in no sense an answer to the conversation Elizabeth and Darcy have been having.[1]

When Caroline Bingley lists the talents of the really accomplished woman, she seems about as hollow as her suggested paragon, and Darcy's way of catching up and elaborating on what she has said effectively serves to dismiss her from the conversation. Caroline has already referred rather snidely to Elizabeth as 'a great reader' (37), though she has hardly included this trait among her list of female 'accomplishments'. Yet there is no doubting the weight Darcy himself attaches to 'extensive reading', which he gives primary importance to. What is, however, hard to catch is the tone of his earlier words: '*All this* she must possess, and to *all this* she must yet add something more substantial' (my italics). Are we to assume that he is endorsing everything in Miss Bingley's list of accomplishments, and that, for reasons which he would find it convenient to adopt, his standards are impossibly high? Or is it that his final words to Elizabeth contain an element of banter: 'Are you so severe upon your own sex, as to doubt the possibility of all this?'

The relationship of Elizabeth and Darcy begins in a haughty aloofness on his side and a readiness to oppose him on hers; yet her constant challenging of him fosters and holds his interest. When at the Lucases' Sir William invites him to dance with Elizabeth but she looks 'archly' (26) and turns away, Darcy disappoints the indefatigable Miss Bingley by saying that he was not silently passing 'strictures' on the assembled company, but instead 'meditating on the very great pleasure which a pair of fine eyes in the face of a pretty woman can bestow' (27). Darcy comes to respond not merely to Elizabeth's 'fine eyes' but to her fine intelligence, and one senses in their conversations at Netherfield, and later at Rosings, how much he welcomes her stimulating presence. When her mother visits Jane at Netherfield and displays to the company her fussy self-importance and shameless want of understanding, Elizabeth takes the conversation on to another plane and has Darcy smile at her wit in opposing the notion that poetry is 'the food of love' (44–5). Indeed, her stimulating presence becomes infinitely more interesting to him than merely conventional pleasures. When, having finished a letter, he asks 'for the indulgence of some music' (51), he takes the opportunity of 'a lively Scotch air' for 'drawing near' her and asking whether she feels like dancing. At this he receives a spirited rebuff. Elizabeth had 'rather expected to affront him . . . but there was a mixture of sweetness and archness in her manner which made it difficult for her to affront anybody', and Darcy, it is said, 'had never been so bewitched by any woman as he was by her' (52).

During their final conversation at Netherfield, many of the points that have already begun to emerge are subtly reinforced and extended; and a further important point is introduced – the implicit connection between intimacy and teasing. Miss Bingley, despite her assertion of that 'certain something' a woman should 'possess', fails to attract Darcy's attention by walking 'about the room' (56), and only succeeds in doing so after she has invited Elizabeth to join her. Yet because of her wheedling coyness she leaves Elizabeth and herself open to hearing Darcy's reasons for not joining them. '"Oh! shocking!" cried Miss Bingley. "I never heard any thing so abominable. How shall we punish him for such a speech?"' (56–7) Elizabeth suggests they should 'teaze him – laugh at him', adding: 'Intimate as you are, you must know how it is to be done.' (57) Miss Bingley, however, who lacks the wit to express herself towards Darcy in such a manner, considers this impossible.

'Mr. Darcy is not to be laughed at!' cried Elizabeth. 'That is an uncommon advantage, and uncommon I hope it will continue, for it would be a great loss to *me* to have many such acquaintance. I dearly love a laugh.'

'Miss Bingley,' said he, 'has given me credit for more than can be. The wisest and the best of men, nay, the wisest and best of their actions, may be rendered ridiculous by a person whose first object in life is a joke.'

'Certainly,' replied Elizabeth – 'there are such people, but I hope I am not one of *them*. I hope I never ridicule what is wise or good. Follies and nonsense, whims and inconsistencies *do* divert me, I own, and I laugh at them whenever I can. – But these, I suppose, are precisely what you are without.'

'Perhaps that is not possible for any one. But it has

been the study of my life to avoid those weaknesses which often expose a strong understanding to ridicule.'

'Such as vanity and pride.'

'Yes, vanity is a weakness indeed. But pride – where there is a real superiority of mind, pride will be always under good regulation.'

Elizabeth turned away to hide a smile.

'Your examination of Mr. Darcy is over, I presume,' said Miss Bingley; – and pray what is the result?'

'I am perfectly convinced by it that Mr. Darcy has no defect. He owns it himself without disguise.'

Elizabeth has, in fact, teased Darcy in a way that reminds us of the derivation of the word. Her words act like a teasel: intended to be pricking to a far greater degree than merely pin-pricking, they tease out and raise the nap on his character. And obviously he finds this both unusual and stimulating. Though it calls forth some seriousness on his part, he is also committed to responding, and may even be felt to do so with a trace of eagerness:

'No' – said Darcy, 'I have made no such pretension. I have faults enough, but they are not, I hope, of understanding. My temper I dare not vouch for. – It is I believe too little yielding – certainly too little for the convenience of the world. I cannot forget the follies and vices of others so soon as I ought, nor their offences against myself. My feelings are not puffed about with every attempt to move them. My temper would perhaps be called resentful. – My good opinion once lost is lost for ever.'

'*That* is a failing indeed!' – cried Elizabeth. 'Implacable resentment *is* a shade in a character. But you have chosen your fault well. – I really cannot *laugh* at it. You are safe from me.'

'There is, I believe, in every disposition a tendency to

42

some particular evil, a natural defect, which not even the best education can overcome.'

'And *your* defect is a propensity to hate every body.'

'And yours,' he replied with a smile, 'is wilfully to misunderstand them' (58).

Elizabeth and Darcy have between them a conversation to which the music Miss Bingley then calls for becomes merely a safe and lesser alternative. Though his friend Bingley has previously tried to answer him by remarks more nearly personal – as when he pictures him as a most 'aweful object' at home of a Sunday evening (50–1) – Elizabeth's spirited rallying of Darcy, accompanied, as it is, by 'a mixture of sweetness and archness in her manner' (52), not merely excites his interest but has the potential for establishing something more like intimacy between them. Even though she later admits to him to never having spoken 'without rather wishing to give [him] pain than not' (380), her words prevent Darcy from taking refuge in arrogance and force him to engage with real questions about himself. They pursue him closely in a manner in which he is willing to be pursued. Again they prompt him to 'smile', which is an indication not so much of his satisfaction at what he has said as of his interest in Elizabeth and in what, above all, has aroused this – the play of wit and intelligence which marks her personality and which he has the discrimination and intelligence to appreciate and respond to. Despite the pride and prejudice on each side, which for so long keep them apart, their conversations together have what only they can share. Elizabeth's lively and challenging remarks arouse his interest in a special way; and in demanding an immediate return, they put him on his mettle.

One thing she holds against him is what she assumes to have been his mistreatment of Wickham, who therefore finds it easy to exploit her prejudice by using insinuation as a means of blackening Darcy's character. Certain signs of incredulity do, as it happens, rise to her lips:

> 'But what . . . can have been his motive? . . . I had not thought Mr. Darcy so bad as this. . . . I wonder that the very pride of this Mr. Darcy has not made him just to you! . . . I am astonished at his intimacy with Mr. Bingley . . . who seems good humour itself' (80–2).

Yet all of these half-formed objections to what she is willingly hearing are most plausibly turned by the son of Pemberley's former steward to his own advantage. Later, enlightened by Darcy's letter, her stance towards Wickham becomes more critical:

> She could see him instantly before her, in every charm of air and address; but she could remember no more substantial good than the general approbation of the neighbourhood, and the regard which his social powers had gained him in the mess (206).

Wickham's 'charm' is at first enough to flatter Elizabeth, but is not substantial enough to engage and hold her attention. She comes to hear him speak with a very different idea of what his abilities are. She is offended by the 'idle and frivolous gallantry' he again tries to show her; yet her disgust also proceeds from a more unvarying source: 'She had even learnt to detect, in the very gentleness which had first delighted her, an affectation and a sameness to disgust and weary' (233). This confirms the view she had earlier come to in mentally putting Wickham beside Darcy's cousin Colonel Fitzwilliam: 'Though, in comparing them, she saw there was less captivating softness in Colonel Fitzwilliam's manners, she believed he might have the best informed mind' (180).

Such a comparison could not at this stage have included Darcy, though Elizabeth's wish to know his character – which has seemed to her so puzzling (93) – causes during their dance at Netherfield a temporary awkwardness between them. He for the moment resents her presumption; yet while it is that, her wish also indicates her latent and even growing interest in him. What it more generally indicates is Elizabeth's sense of something much deeper than surfaces. Though not above making mistakes, and though always willing to give so much of herself, she cannot give herself wholly where there is anything less than mutual respect or trust. Here there is a difference between Elizabeth and her former close friend Charlotte Lucas. Talking of Bingley and Jane, Charlotte says,

> 'I should think she had as good a chance of happiness, as if she were to be studying his character for a twelve-month. Happiness in marriage is entirely a matter of chance. . . . It is better to know as little as possible of the defects of the person with whom you are to pass your life' (23).

Elizabeth, however, will have none of this: 'You make me laugh, Charlotte; but it is not sound. You know it is not sound, and that you would never act in this way yourself.'

In marrying Mr Collins Charlotte does act in this way. While Elizabeth does not give Collins a moment's thought, Charlotte's apparently self-interested action means that her friend can never be really close to her again. Not only is Charlotte by this action 'sunk in her esteem' (125), but Elizabeth knows 'no real confidence' can 'ever subsist between them again' (128). After Charlotte is married, though they continue their correspondence, it is 'impossible' that 'it should be equally unreserved': 'Elizabeth could never address her without feeling that all the comfort of intimacy was over' (146). She will not allow Charlotte to have 'a proper way of thinking' in intending to marry Collins, and will not let Jane excuse her by changing 'the meaning of principle and integrity' (135–6).

Elizabeth is, moreover, annoyed by the letter her sister has received from Caroline Bingley, who boasts so 'joyfully' of the 'increasing intimacy' of Miss Darcy and herself (133). In a spirit of some disillusionment she says, 'There are few people whom I really love, and still fewer of whom I think well' (135). Yet a comment such as this at least reinforces our sense of what would be necessary to earn the return of Elizabeth's love.

In Elizabeth's first, surprised reaction to Charlotte's news, she is unguarded enough to exclaim upon it, so that her friend replies in a way that means the intimacy which has existed between them must come to an end. What follows acknowledges as much: Elizabeth, given the change in the situation, can no longer speak to her friend with real warmth or directness. Yet this kind of stand-off never really occurs between Darcy and herself. His reaction to the telling things she says about him ensures that their conversation will be full of mutual interest. Indeed it is this which gives to it the potential for something more – for an intimacy which is out of the ordinary even though it still has to be acknowledged as a process of mutual sharing.

When they meet again at Rosings, we are inevitably reminded of what has earlier passed between them. Their conversation in Lady Catherine de Bourgh's drawing room is one of the high points of the novel. It has its origin in Elizabeth's spirited reaction (or over-reaction) to Darcy's presence, and it issues, not surprisingly, in some overstatement on her part. On Darcy's stationing himself near her at the piano, 'so as to command a full view of the fair performer's countenance', Elizabeth turns to him 'with an arch smile' and says,

> 'You mean to frighten me, Mr. Darcy, by coming in all this state to hear me? But I will not be alarmed though your sister *does* play so well. There is a stubbornness

about me that never can bear to be frightened at the will of others' (174).

Darcy recognises the element of exaggeration in this; yet there is also an element of truth in what she says. Elizabeth does not permit her 'will' to be dictated to by another, and she will never admit the submissive role traditionally ascribed to women, which, in Chesterfield's words, specified that they should 'be talked to as below men, and above children'.[2] It is in Darcy's favour that he sublim- inally recognises the value of Elizabeth's conversation. Any intimacy they will share can only develop from a situation of equality. Though Darcy does not acknowl- edge this in the manner of his proposal, he at least implicitly recognises it when Elizabeth so closely searches his character.

Among Lady Catherine's first questions to Elizabeth are, 'Do you play and sing, Miss Bennet?' and, 'Do your sisters play and sing?' (164); and it is surely no accident that so many of the important scenes in the first half of the novel take place around the piano. What follows from these is a continuing revaluation of the conventional notion of 'performance' and 'accomplishments'. When Elizabeth, under the guise of being in a position to relate such things of Darcy as would 'shock' (174) his relations, mentions not Wickham but his dancing 'only four dances' at a ball, even though to her 'certain knowledge, more than one young lady was sitting down in want of a partner' (175), Darcy makes some weak attempts to excuse himself. Elizabeth, however, does not let the matter rest there. Having applied to Fitzwilliam for a reason why 'a man of sense and education, and who has lived in the world, is ill qualified to recommend himself to strangers', she gets this unequivocal answer: 'It is because he will not give himself the trouble.' Though Darcy again tries to explain, saying, 'I certainly have not the talent which some people possess of conversing easily with those I have never seen before', Elizabeth now has the means of pushing her point home:

> 'My fingers', said Elizabeth, 'do not move over this instrument in the masterly manner which I see so many women's do. They have not the same force or rapidity, and do not produce the same expression. But then I have always supposed it to be my own fault – because I would not take the trouble of practising. It is not that I do not believe *my* fingers as capable as any other woman's of superior execution.'

Jane Austen has brilliantly contrived this scene by interweaving the remarks on music and 'manner' (or manners): 'True; and nobody can ever be introduced in a ball room. Well, Colonel Fitzwilliam, what do I play next? My fingers wait your orders.' Elizabeth is not so much being pert as pertinent. The point she goes on to make is related to what Lady Catherine has said about the importance of 'practising'. It also arises beautifully apropos from her being seated at the piano. And the response it calls forth from Darcy explicitly acknowledges the limitations of the conventional view of the accomplished woman:

> Darcy smiled and said, 'You are perfectly right. You have employed your time much better. No one admitted to the privilege of hearing you, can think any thing wanting. We neither of us perform to strangers' (176).

Not only are Darcy's words a well-disguised admission that Elizabeth has made a real point, but they indicate the high value he places on her conversation. What he acknowledges is that there is a more intrinsic kind of excellence which she as a woman has cultivated to the full, and which is a matter, not of musical prowess, or of superficial or extrinsic 'accomplishments', but of conver-

sational powers and intelligence, and, indeed, the culti-
vation of the whole person. His words, in reflecting back
on the kind of education his aunt had assumed the Bennet
girls should have had, vindicate the use Elizabeth herself
has made of the 'means' that were open to her. As she had
said to Lady Catherine, 'Such of us as wished to learn,
never wanted the means. We were always encouraged to
read, and had all the masters that were necessary' (165).
The slight hint of knowing irony in Darcy's words, 'We
neither of us perform to strangers', also continues that
element of serious banter which, on his side, he seems to
recognise as existing between them. As he places Elizabeth
and himself in the same company, he subtly draws
attention, not only to her 'performance' in such a
gathering, but to what he has found most fascinating
about her. There is, then, a tantalising privacy about his
closing words. He expects her to realise that these are also
directed at herself; but any conscious irony is almost
totally subsumed in his larger and more significant
acknowledgement.

Darcy's words contain, however, irony of another kind.
In her first conversation with Wickham, Elizabeth had
been sufficiently unreserved:

> 'Are you much acquainted with Mr. Darcy?'
> 'As much as I ever wish to be', cried Elizabeth
> warmly, – 'I have spent four days in the same house
> with him, and I think him very disagreeable' (77).

Wickham had slyly hinted at being a virtual stranger
before whom Elizabeth might not choose to express
herself openly; yet this implied challenging of her had led
her to be even more assertive:

> 'Upon my word I say no more *here* than I might say in
> any house in the neighbourhood, except Netherfield.
> He is not at all liked in Hertfordshire. Every body is

disgusted with his pride. You will not find him more favourably spoken of by any one' (77–8).

After, however, she has received Darcy's letter, Elizabeth is bound to reflect on her earlier conversation with Wickham:

> Many of his expressions were still fresh in her memory, She was *now* struck with the impropriety of such communications to a stranger, and wondered it had escaped her before. She saw the indelicacy of putting himself forward as he had done, and the inconsistency of his professions with his conduct (206–7).

Though it is Wickham's 'impropriety' which strikes her, Elizabeth comes to entertain no favourable impression of her own conduct:

> She grew absolutely ashamed of herself. – Of neither Darcy nor Wickham could she think, without feeling that she had been blind, partial, prejudiced, absurd.
>
> 'How despicably have I acted!' she cried. – 'I, who have prided myself on my discernment! – I, who have valued myself on my abilities! who have often disdained the generous candour of my sister, and gratified my vanity, in useless or blameable distrust. – How humiliating is this discovery!' (208)

Her self-reproaches do not specifically include her own 'impropriety', but they occur on the occasion when she has also to consider and acknowledge the force of that 'total want of propriety' which Darcy had 'so frequently' noticed among certain members of her family (198). She has already criticised Charlotte for not possessing 'a proper way of thinking' in agreeing to marry Collins. What she has herself to achieve is 'a proper way of thinking' about Wickham and Darcy – something which her own outspokenness has seemed to hinder. She has therefore a lesson to learn, as she readily enough acknowledges.

If Elizabeth needs to question her own behaviour, the same is true of Darcy, who provokes her most by the manner of his proposal. While his sentiments are often impeccable, they also appear stilted, even stiff-necked, until a close encounter with Elizabeth prompts him to take on a certain sparkle. In some ways he needs to forget himself long enough to accord her fitting attention. And that she persuades him to do this argues her personal vitality and intelligence.

The final sentence of the second volume of the novel – 'To Pemberley, therefore, they were to go' (241) – has an air of expectancy about it, and it is in the third volume that we meet a thoroughly changed Darcy and Elizabeth experiences a new world. On viewing Pemberley, Elizabeth is surprised by the high praise his housekeeper gives him, but she is also conscious of its value: 'What praise is more valuable than the praise of an intelligent servant?' (250).[3] Moreover, though she is herself acutely embarrassed in unexpectedly meeting him again, she is also surprised to find that his 'manners' are so 'softened' (255); while her uncle declares him to be 'perfectly well behaved, polite, and unassuming' (257). Elizabeth sees Pemberley before she again meets Darcy, but that she does so with 'spirits . . . in a high flutter' (245) is attributable to what she has begun to feel for him. The place itself nevertheless impresses her; and, in the best country-house tradition, this is not unconnected with its being an expression of its owner:

> She had never seen a place for which nature had done
> more, or where natural beauty had been so little
> counteracted by an awkward taste. . . . Every dispo-
> sition of the ground was good; and she looked on the
> whole scene, the river, the trees scattered on its banks,
> and the winding of the valley, as far as she could trace it,
> with delight. As they passed into other rooms, these

objects were taking different positions; but from every window there were beauties to be seen. The rooms were lofty and handsome, and their furniture suitable to the fortune of their proprietor; but Elizabeth saw, with admiration of his taste, that it was neither gaudy nor uselessly fine; with less of splendor, and more real elegance, than the furniture of Rosings (245–6).

The meeting of Elizabeth and Darcy at Pemberley is an awkward one for both of them. Her sense of 'the impropriety of her being found there' (252) co-exists, when he has withdrawn, with her intense interest in what he is thinking and feeling:

> Her thoughts were all fixed on that one spot of Pemberley House, whichever it might be, where Mr. Darcy then was. She longed to know what at that moment was passing in his mind; in what manner he thought of her, and whether, in defiance of every thing, she was still dear to him. Perhaps he had been civil, only because he felt himself at ease; yet there had been *that* in his voice, which was not like ease. Whether he had felt more of pain or of pleasure in seeing her, she could not tell, but he certainly had not seen her with composure (253).

When Darcy reappears, extends to her uncle an invitation to fish his stream, and asks Elizabeth to be permitted to introduce his sister to her, the reader is left in no doubt (though Elizabeth cannot presume to be confident of it) that he still loves her. The awkwardness on each side as they wait for the Gardiners is evident from the difficulty they find in conversing together, for 'there seemed an embargo on every subject' (257). Finally, they talk 'of Matlock and Dove Dale with great perseverance'.

However traditional it was to regard love as a civilising force, the change from the Darcy of his initial appearance is most marked. Even though Mrs Gardiner notes 'something a little stately in him' and pronounces it 'not unbecoming' (257), she and her husband are aware that 'had they drawn his character from their own feelings, and his servant's report . . . the circle in Hertfordshire to which he was known, would not have recognised it for Mr. Darcy' (264). In particular we remember the Darcy who regards Bingley's sisters as the only women in the room 'whom it would not be a punishment . . . to stand up with' (11), or who 'coldly' says of Elizabeth: 'She is tolerable; but not handsome enough to tempt *me*' (12). While the novel is something of a *tour de force*, in seeking to metamorphose Darcy's 'pride' from something repulsive to something we can almost forgive, our sense of what Elizabeth and Darcy will eventually share is not based merely on the altered feelings that each displays on meeting again in Derbyshire. Though Elizabeth's 'deeper sentiment of gratitude' at Darcy's 'regard' (251) is increased by his efforts to preserve Lydia's social respectability in having Wickham marry her, what has earlier passed between them reappears with a new sparkle towards the end of the novel.

When, however, Darcy comes to Longbourn, Elizabeth has some distressing moments. She is 'astonished and vexed' when he sits silent and reserved, saying to herself, 'If he no longer cares for me, why silent? Teazing, teazing, man! I will think no more about him' (339). Of course, Darcy is not deliberately setting out to tease Elizabeth: as he later explains, he was 'embarrassed' (381) and, given the strength of his feelings for her, unable to converse with ease; but because of what Elizabeth has come to feel for him, his silence is teasing in the extreme. It presents the kind of challenge which she cannot get the better of, much as her own conversation had done to Darcy. Later, when all is settled between them, though her attitude to Darcy has long since changed, her latent challenging of him continues to draw them together. Even in the post-mortem they hold on earlier feelings and events, though each has a need to be – and even enjoys being – serious and self-critical, there is often a liveliness in Elizabeth's words that is just below the surface.

A hint of this can be seen in her response to Darcy's hope that she does not have 'the power' of reading again the opening of his letter: 'The letter shall certainly be burnt, if you believe it essential to the preservation of my regard' (368). When Darcy has explained to her why he was so 'grave and silent' on meeting her again, Elizabeth replies, 'How unlucky that you should have a reasonable answer to give, and that I should be so reasonable as to admit it' (381). Such a remark proves that she is in no danger of making the kind of 'unequal marriage' which her father at first fears she might make in marrying someone she cannot 'respect' (376), for Elizabeth would be unable to respond to a man in this way unless she both respected his intelligence and felt confident of his appreciation in return. Such good-humoured teasing is meant to be pleasantly provoking, and to this extent is in fact covertly sexual.

This important side of their future relationship can also be glimpsed through the eyes of Darcy's sister:

Georgiana had the highest opinion in the world of Elizabeth; though at first she often listened with an astonishment bordering on alarm, at her lively, sportive, manner of talking to her brother. He, who had always inspired in herself a respect which almost overcame her affection, she now saw the object of open pleasantry. Her mind received knowledge which had never before fallen in her way. By Elizabeth's instructions she began to comprehend that a woman may take liberties with her husband, which a brother will not always allow in a sister more than ten years younger than himself (387–8).

The relationship of Elizabeth and Darcy is as solidly based as this, the natural outgrowth of a mutual interest and responsiveness that has been theirs almost from the outset. Nothing comparable could have been excited had Elizabeth possessed merely conventional 'accomplishments', and she rightly declares her intention of continuing in the manner (if not in the spirit) she has begun. When Darcy praises her 'affectionate behaviour to Jane', Elizabeth replies:

> 'Dearest Jane! who could have done less for her? But make a virtue of it by all means. My good qualities are under your protection, and you are to exaggerate them as much as possible; and, in return, it belongs to me to find occasions for teazing and quarrelling with you as often as may be' (381).

It has been suggested of Jane Austen that 'the conscious giving up of passion' is 'the price her heroines pay for "consciousness"', and that Elizabeth Bennet, who 'rather *knew* herself to be happy, than *felt* herself to be so' (372), exemplifies this tendency.[4] Whatever truth there is, however, in the related suggestion that the author was aware of the psychological threat of sexuality to 'the certainties of self-hood and identity',[5] neither the immediate context in *Pride and Prejudice*, nor the larger context of Elizabeth and Darcy's relationship, bears out the above interpretation of Elizabeth's state of mind. Rather, she is apprehensive of 'what would be felt in the family when her situation became known; she was aware that no one liked him but Jane.' Moreover, even when her family and her Meryton relations know of her engagement to Darcy, Elizabeth is unable to relax into a genuine intimacy with him because of the 'vulgar' attentions of those present:

Elizabeth . . . was ever anxious to keep him to herself, and to those of her family with whom he might converse without mortification; and though the uncomfortable feelings arising from all this took from the season of courtship much of its pleasure, it added to the hope of the future; and she looked forward with delight to the time when they should be removed from society so little pleasing to either, to all the comfort and elegance of their family party at Pemberley (384).

The very thing that attracts Darcy to Elizabeth is what gives the lie to the suggestion that she needs to abandon her individual 'consciousness' in order to find happiness with him. When she rather provokingly asks, 'Did you admire me for my impertinence?' (380), he aptly replies, 'For the liveliness of your mind, I did.' Conventional 'accomplishments', whether as a means of defence or allurement, form no part of her make-up or intentions. Instead she expresses her quintessential self in her conversational exchanges with him. One striking example of the playfulness of her wit occurs when she herself makes this very point:

'You were disgusted with the women who were always speaking and looking, and thinking for *your* approbation alone. I roused, and interested you, because I was so unlike *them*. Had you not been really amiable you would have hated me for it; but in spite of the pains you took to disguise yourself, your feelings were always noble and just; and in your heart, you thoroughly despised the persons who so assiduously courted you. There – I have saved you the trouble of accounting for it; and really, all things considered, I begin to think it perfectly reasonable. To be sure, you knew no actual good of me – but nobody thinks of *that* when they fall in love.'

Here Elizabeth gives even Darcy's earlier behaviour a handsome and affectionate gloss, without giving up, moreover, the delight of still teasing him. By her behaviour she fashions him into a fitting companion for herself, for Darcy has the discrimination and responsiveness to rise to the challenge. Obviously he will continue to find her as bewitching and fascinating as he ever did.

Fanny Price

Among the marriages anticipated for the heroines of Jane Austen's novels, how convincing is that of Edmund Bertram and Fanny Price? On the face of it, the question needs to be asked because the author's attempt to explain their 'happiness' sounds rather hollow:

> With so much true merit and true love, and no want of fortune or friends, the happiness of the married cousins must appear as secure as earthly happiness can be. – Equally formed for domestic life, and attached to country pleasures, their home was the home of affection and comfort . . . (473).

It is, moreover, in the last chapter of the novel that we come across this description of Edmund: 'After wandering about and sitting under trees with Fanny all the summer evenings, he had so well talked his mind into submission, as to be very tolerably cheerful again ' (462). What begins as their lengthy conversation about Mary Crawford ends by his 'being always' with Fanny 'and always talking confidentially' – which amounts to his dawning realisation that 'a very different kind of woman' from Mary 'might . . . do just as well, or a great deal better' (470). Given that the coming together of these two characters is made explicit in these terms, how confident are we invited to be of their future 'happiness'?

What Julia Brown, in writing of the novel, has aptly

referred to as its 'Victorian anxieties', its 'uncanny sensation of closeness yet distance',[1] is not as simple to account for as traditional criticism of Fanny might suggest. Though Mrs Austen thought her 'insipid', and Kingsley Amis has reviled her as 'a monster of complacency and pride' operating 'under a cloak of cringing self-abasement',[2] Fanny is, as we shall see, a more interesting and more sympathetic character than such comments allow. Her inability to communicate with others is in some sense forced upon her, not merely by her own situation and temperament, but by the exigencies of the plot. Moreover, Edmund, while attentive to her needs, does not engage with her nature in any more intimate way. Indeed he comes closest to doing so only when he wishes to confide in her his love for another. This not only argues his insensitiveness to her deeper needs, but effectively precludes the dynamics of a relationship in which a more genuine intimacy can develop between them.

The emptiness that can follow from insensitivity is pointedly caricatured in the incidental description of what Maria Bertram suffers in Mr Rushworth's company:

> Maria, with only Mr. Rushworth to attend to her, and doomed to the repeated details of his day's sport, good or bad, his boast of his dogs, his jealousy of his neighbours, his doubts of their qualification, and his zeal after poachers, – subjects which will not find their way to female feelings without some talent on one side, or some attachment on the other, had missed Mr. Crawford grievously (115).

Edmund, of course, is partly conscious of Fanny's unassuming yet genuine responsiveness. In discussing her proposed removal to Mrs Norris, he says to her:

> 'There is no reason in the world why you should not be important where you are known. You have good sense,

and a sweet temper, and I am sure you have a grateful heart, that could never receive kindness without wishing to return it. I do not know any better qualifications for a friend and companion' (26).

Yet, even though, as her foster-brother, Edmund would not have thought of the youthful Fanny more seriously than this, when she has become a woman, and comes to be noticed by others, there still seems a barrier to a more reciprocal relationship between them. In part this is to be accounted for by his preoccupation with Mary Crawford; nevertheless, there also seems a curious blindness on his part not just to Mary's faults but to Fanny's virtues.

Edmund is captivated by Mary's liveliness, and even Fanny at first finds her an attractive personality, admitting that she likes 'to hear her talk' and has 'great pleasure in looking at her' (63). There are moments in the novel when Mary indeed seems winning, as when she consoles Fanny after Mrs Norris's shameless attack on her, or bids her an affectionate farewell on leaving Mansfield. Even her occasional remarks can be enlivening; for example, after Fanny has 'turned farther into the window' on receiving a compliment from Edmund, Mary says, 'I fancy Miss Price has been more used to deserve praise than to hear it' (112). Sometimes, though we are made aware of the author's condemnation, we glimpse Mary's keen fascination with life. Writing of Henry's presumed presence at Mrs Fraser's party, she adds, 'He will see the Rushworths, which I own I am not sorry for – having a little curiosity – and so I think has he, though he will not acknowledge it' (417).

Yet Edmund is also disturbed by certain things Mary says. When she speaks 'freely' of her uncle the admiral, Edmund falls silent (57); and her liveliness makes him feel 'grave' when she indecorously draws attention to her professedly unconscious pun: 'Certainly, my home at my uncle's brought me acquainted with a circle of admirals.

Of *Rears*, and *Vices*, I saw enough. Now, do not be suspecting me of a pun, I entreat' (60). Here there seems some justification for the way Jane Austen measures Mary off against her heroine: 'Miss Crawford was very unlike her. She had none of Fanny's delicacy of taste, of mind, of feeling' (81). Not merely is there sometimes a trace of heedlessness or even vulgarity in what Mary says; there is also the suggestion of her contempt for what Edmund holds so dear. In the chapel at Sotherton, she indulges in this witty sally against the practice of family prayers:

> 'It must do the heads of the family a great deal of good to force all the poor housemaids and footmen to leave business and pleasure, and say their prayers here twice a day, while they are inventing excuses themselves for staying away. . . . Cannot you imagine with what unwilling feelings the former belles of the house of Rushworth did many a time repair to this chapel? The young Mrs. Eleanors and Mrs. Bridgets – starched up into seeming piety, but with heads full of something very different – especially if the poor chaplain were not worth looking at – and, in those days, I fancy parsons were very inferior even to what they are now' (86–7).

Mary does not yet know that Edmund intends to be a clergyman. When she finds out, she quickly recovers to say, 'If I had known this before, I would have spoken of the cloth with more respect' (89). Yet Mary is never able to reconcile herself to Edmund's choice of profession, for she is never able to admit what she would consider a loss of significance in her own eyes.

For some reason that seems bound up with this, Edmund finds it difficult to converse with Mary in a mutually satisfying way. These two young people seem unable to talk as lovers until they rehearse their roles as Amelia and Anhalt in *Lovers' Vows*. There the words are determined for them in a kind of surrogate courtship, so that they can, in a sense, lose themselves in their parts. They rise to a level of animation and even naturalness that is clearly not theirs when they are not thus 'acting' the role of lovers; yet, despite this, when Fanny, 'agitated by the increasing spirit of Edmund's manner', closes 'the page' (170), he is unable to continue without prompting. This may be seen as almost symbolic, as though Fanny's presence is integral to his needs. At the same time, in the role of prompter, she is forced to experience in a vicarious way what must inevitably give her pain.

It is not only Mary's attitude to the cloth that makes her seem unsuitable for Edmund. Sometimes, despite the attractiveness that her liveliness engenders, the reader is invited to be more discriminating than Edmund for much of the novel is capable of being. There is a hint of opportunism in Mary's make-up, and she admits to selfishness in keeping Fanny waiting for her ride:

'My dear Miss Price,' said Miss Crawford, as soon as she was at all within hearing, 'I am come to make my own apologies for keeping you waiting – but I have nothing in the world to say for myself – I knew it was very late, and that I was behaving extremely ill; and, therefore, if you please, you must forgive me. Selfishness must always be forgiven you know, because there is no hope of a cure' (68).

Nor is there any mistaking how naked Mary's self-interest can be when jealousy overtakes her. Feeling the Owen sisters to be a threat, since Edmund is spending some time with their family, Mary gives expression to thoughts of a mercenary and reductive kind:

'Stranger things have happened. I dare say they are trying for it. And they are quite in the right, for it would be a very pretty establishment for them. I do not at all

wonder or blame them. – It is every body's duty to do as
well for themselves as they can' (289).

Even though we occasionally feel that the author is not
behaving quite fairly to Mary Crawford, we are finally left
with an impression of some disingenuousness.[3] Mary's
remarks at the ball to Sir Thomas, Lady Bertram, Mrs
Norris and Fanny are trimmed for every hearer, though
'she blundered most towards Fanny herself, in her
intentions to please' (277). There is, too, a suggestion of
pretence in her assuming that Fanny must know why
Henry goes to town – for she has still to learn that her
brother is serious about Fanny instead of merely playing at
making her love him. This makes the collusion between
the Crawfords over the necklace less pardonable than it
might otherwise have seemed. Even at the time, though
Fanny tries to feel sincere in her obligation, Mary's words
make her uneasy: '"You must think of somebody else too
when you wear that necklace," replied Miss Crawford.
"You must think of Henry, for it was his choice in the first
place"' (259). Fanny notices 'an expression in Miss
Crawford's eyes which she could not be satisfied with'
(260). While she is not inclined to show Mary an
affectionate regard, there is, we learn, reason for her
entertaining the view that 'Miss Crawford, complaisant as
a sister, was careless as a woman and a friend'.

By contrast with Mary, Fanny's responsiveness is to
people and values, and what the young Maria and Julia
regard as a sign of their little cousin's stupidity is
thoroughly characteristic of the woman she becomes.
When they ask her 'which way she would go to get to
Ireland' (18), Fanny thinks only of the Isle of Wight as the
one 'island' which, lying off Portsmouth, has a special
place in her affections. Moreover, as well as having a
nature that feels things acutely, she also has a fine sense of
discrimination. While often seeming something of a

bystander, as during the visit to Sotherton or the constant rehearsing of *Lovers' Vows*, Fanny's perceptions reflect a keen insight into what is going on around her. In the interior consciousness of her silences, not merely her tremulousness is opened to us. Only she, for example, notices and pities the rejection Julia suffers over the casting of the play: 'They were two solitary sufferers, or connected only by Fanny's consciousness' (163). Fanny's consciousness also extends to the very substance of what Jane Austen sees holds human relationships together. When she imagines – certainly not as 'independently of self' as she believes – that the 'increasing attachment' between Edmund and Mary will be enough to 'unite them' (367), she is nevertheless aware of the lack of some more common basis for sharing. Mary, she believes, 'might love', but does not 'deserve Edmund by any other sentiment'; 'Fanny believed there was scarcely a second feeling in common between them.' While Fanny recognises the strength of the attraction they feel for each other, her own deeper feeling towards Edmund enables her to see that Mary in no way engages with those other qualities which define for Fanny his essential nature. An obvious example of this is Mary's failure to understand the seriousness of Edmund's commitment to being ordained; but ultimately a more telling example is her inability to comprehend that the grave indiscretion of her brother and Maria Rushworth cannot be countenanced as merely 'folly' (454).

Though Fanny feels keenly Edmund's growing attachment to Mary, she never allows herself to be drawn into an open discussion of her character. The reader nevertheless senses Fanny's unspoken commentary on Mary, not least because she is unable to follow where Edmund would have her go. Moreover, the grouping of Fanny and Mary frequently indicates how diametrically opposed they are. When they dine together at the park, Fanny sits 'on the

other side of Edmund, exactly opposite Miss Crawford'
(56). During the evening they all spend together following
the trip to Sotherton, Mary again raises the question of
Edmund's choosing to take orders, and after a time moves
away from him and Fanny to join the others in a glee at the
piano. For a while Fanny manages to keep him with her at
the open window, and, moved by the beauty of the night,
hopes he will go outside with her to look at the stars. But
as the glee gets under way, Edmund, 'turning his back on
the window', gradually leaves Fanny in order to move
closer to the singers, and becomes 'among the most urgent
in requesting to hear the glee again' (113).

This brief scene is suggestive, not merely in the rare
moment it captures of potential intimacy, but in providing
an implicit contrast with the very different aura that
surrounds Mary Crawford. It therefore meshes with our
sense of an opposition – almost of different worlds – that
occurs in the fabric of this novel. Standing with Edmund
at the window, Fanny denies that she would be 'afraid' of
venturing out on to the lawn to see more of the night sky.
The privacy afforded by 'the brilliancy of an unclouded
night' (113) seems altogether more accommodating than
the episode at Sotherton or the riding parties around
Mansfield, which occur in the glare of day and suggest an
element of unrestrained self-gratification. Fanny and
Edmund look out on a world that seems momentarily to
take them out of themselves with a consciousness of what
they can share – a potential responsiveness very different
from the apparent contrivance of Mary in that earlier scene
when she is 'placed near a window, cut down to the
ground' with 'a harp as elegant as herself' (65). By
succumbing to the 'glee', Edmund, however, seems less in
possession of himself, and when he moves 'forward'
towards it 'by gentle degrees', he turns his back on what
has flowed momentarily between Fanny and himself for an
apparently unthinking devotion to present pleasure.

A similar movement from Fanny to Mary occurs during the casting of *Lovers' Vows*. At first Edmund stands out with Fanny against what Sir Thomas is later to regard as their 'unsafe amusements' (188) during his absence. When, however, no Anhalt can be found to play opposite Mary's Amelia, and Tom Bertram proposes going outside the immediate group to approach one or two young men who live nearby, Edmund is persuaded to change his stand. The interview he seeks with Fanny to explain this change of position reveals both his growing tendency to rationalise and her staunch refusal to compromise by departing from what she takes to be the path of virtue:

> 'Put yourself in Miss Crawford's place, Fanny. Consider what it would be to act Amelia with a stranger. She has a right to be felt for, because she evidently feels for herself. I heard enough of what she said to you last night, to understand her unwillingness to be acting with a stranger; and as she probably engaged in the part with different expectations – perhaps, without considering the subject enough to know what was likely to be, it would be ungenerous, it would be really wrong to expose her to it. Her feelings ought to be respected. Does not it strike you so, Fanny? You hesitate.'
>
> 'I am sorry for Miss Crawford; but I am more sorry to see you drawn in to do what you had resolved against, and what you are known to think will be disagreeable to my uncle' (154–5).

Edmund may be putting too sensitive a construction on what Mary has said, for we feel it has been said in part for him to hear. Yet such an exchange alerts us to what Juliet McMaster has noticed as 'one of the major subsurface movements of the novel', namely, 'Edmund's unconscious courtship of Fanny, which is concurrent with his deliberate courtship of Mary'.[4] The different paths this involves him in are, however, singularly divergent, and sometimes this forces him into a kind of somersault. When Fanny thanks him for the chain he gives her to wear with William's gift of an amber cross, Edmund says, 'Believe me, I have no pleasure in the world superior to that of contributing to yours. No, I can safely say, I have no pleasure so complete, so unalloyed. It is without a drawback' (262). But Fanny is not at this point Edmund's chief 'pleasure' for her account of Mary's giving her the necklace so 'struck' and 'delighted' him 'that Fanny could not but admit the superior power of *one* pleasure over his own mind'. Here Mary seems to stand for Pleasure itself, just as, within a page or two, after Fanny has heard him speak of his great affection for Mary – less 'tolerable' (264) because she believes her not to deserve him – she must, in the manner of Pleasure's traditional opposite, resolve to 'endeavour to be rational', to reveal 'a sound intellect and an honest heart' (265).

Often during the novel Mary seems to radiate or surround herself with 'pleasure'. To adapt her brother's phrase, 'the loss of present pleasure' (84) is what the Crawfords try to avoid. At Sotherton the active Mary, whom only 'resting fatigues' (96), thrives more as she gets further from the house, deeper into 'all the sweets of pleasure-grounds' (90). This episode has been called 'the finest and most original in the Austen novels', with a 'wonderfully sustained but never obtrusive symbolism' and an 'action' that is 'a pregnant microcosm'.[5] While the Miss Bertrams have never yet seen 'the wilderness' (90), it proves to be 'a good spot for fault-finding', and we gain proleptic hints of what will befall Henry and Maria. Yet what has not been noticed is the peculiarly suggestive relationship of the grouping here of Edmund, Mary and Fanny, who 'seemed as naturally to unite' as Maria, Henry and Mr Rushworth. The three characters become for a time physically joined – an emblem of their entanglement and attraction for one another that has to be progressively sorted out throughout the novel. Edmund walks with Fanny's arm drawn 'within his' (94), and with Mary on his other arm. It seems the most natural thing in the world, with Fanny tired and needing support, and Mary needing no such support but taking his arm nevertheless: 'She took it, however, as she spoke, and the gratification of having her do so, of feeling such a connection for the first time, made him a little forgetful of Fanny.' Edmund cannot give them both his undivided attention, and he finally has to choose (however unconsciously) between them.

Later Fanny, left on her own, tries to warn Maria of the danger she is exposing herself to by (at Henry's suggestion) impatiently entering the park without waiting for Rushworth to return with the key to the gate: '"You will hurt yourself, Miss Bertram," she cried, "you will certainly hurt yourself against those spikes – you will tear your gown – you will be in danger of slipping into the ha-ha"' (99–100). Though the world will come to pass a scornful judgment on Maria, even Edmund pays no heed to Fanny when she tries to tell him of her fears. On the Crawfords' arrival at Mansfield, it is said that 'their acquaintance soon promised as early an intimacy as good manners would warrant' (44). Yet it is Fanny's concern at the prospect of intimacy of a dangerous kind that prompts her to hint her fears: '"If Miss Bertram were not engaged," said Fanny, cautiously, "I could sometimes almost think that he admired her more than Julia."' (116). The manner in which Edmund dismisses this suggestion not only demonstrates his misconception of that more inward and subtle kind of intimacy which enables two people to share each other's thoughts and feelings, but also shows how far he is from sharing any such intimacy with Fanny herself:

'Which is, perhaps, more in favour of his liking Julia best, than you, Fanny, may be aware; for I believe it often happens, that a man, before he has quite made up his own mind, will distinguish the sister or intimate friend of the woman he is really thinking of, more than the woman herself.'

Edmund seems to have a wish, not of drawing closer to Fanny, but of having her drawn closer to Mary:

> A friendship between two so very dear to him was exactly what he could have wished; and to the credit of the lover's understanding be it stated, that he did not by any means consider Fanny as the only, or even as the greater gainer by such a friendship (211).

Edmund always champions Fanny both in considering her obvious feelings and wishes, and in acknowledging something of her true worth; and she in turn feeds on his 'looks' and 'kindness' (370). Even so, it is sometimes suggested that he does not take her sufficiently on her own terms, especially when his attitude towards her seems refracted through his desire of seeking a closer association with Mary. On one occasion he speaks to her in a manner that seems tinged with Mary's own style. When Fanny admits to taking pleasure in her uncle's conversation, adding, 'but then I am unlike other people I dare say', Edmund replies in these terms:

> 'Why should you dare say *that*? (smiling) – Do you want to be told that you are only unlike other people in being more wise and discreet? But when did you or any body ever get a compliment from me, Fanny? Go to my father if you want to be complimented. He will satisfy you' (197).

Edmund's attitude is shaped by his own involvement with Mary, though we see most glaringly in the scene between the two young women in Mrs Grant's shrubbery how impossible it is that they should ever really meet. Fanny, reflective and intelligent, is eagerly responsive to her surroundings and speaks interestingly and movingly of the operations of 'memory' (208–9). But Mary remains 'untouched and inattentive', and characteristically considers her surroundings only as they affect herself: 'To say the truth . . . I see no wonder in this shrubbery equal to seeing myself in it' (209–10).

Such intimacy as involves a mutual sharing demands some correspondence of mental and moral capacities, and it is not therefore 'the sort of intimacy' (207) that Fanny and Mary can share. Nor is it the sort of intimacy which, despite Henry Crawford's determined wooing of Fanny, she is ever capable of sharing with him. Only Edmund has the inner qualities that could appreciate this, but he is so blinded by his affection for Mary that one of his more distressing lapses is his failure to grasp why Fanny objects to Henry. During this prolonged episode, the heroine is even more isolated from those who normally wish her well, with the result that the principles she chooses to live by are thoroughly tested. These nevertheless remain unimpaired, and provide the means of allowing us to estimate Henry's character even more clearly.

When Sir Thomas attempts to confide in Fanny, he is unable to account for her attitude to Henry because the implications of a remark such as this quite escape him: 'I told him without disguise that it was very disagreeable to me, and quite out of my power to return his good opinion' (314). Nor is Sir Thomas able to ask the most revealing question:

'Have you any reason, child, to think ill of Mr. Crawford's temper?'
'No, Sir.'
She longed to add, 'but of his principles I have;' but her heart sunk under the appalling prospect of discussion, explanation, and probably non-conviction. Her

ill opinion of him was founded chiefly on observations, which, for her cousins' sake, she could scarcely dare mention to their father (317–18).

Her 'uncle's anger' (321) gives Fanny 'the severest pain of all', and she wishes that 'her only friend' were not absent. But when Edmund returns and talks to her of the matter, she finds it impossible to make even him understand.

Fanny seems to know from the outset how fruitless their talk will be. Some 'comfort' does nevertheless flow from Edmund's agreeing that she has done 'exactly' as she ought – given that she does not love Henry, to whom she has 'not had time' (347) in his view to attach herself. But when he supposes she must feel 'gratitude' towards Henry and therefore have 'the *wish* to love him', Fanny is bound to reply,

> 'We are so totally unlike . . . we are so very, very different in all our inclinations and ways, that I consider it as quite impossible we should ever be tolerably happy together, even if I *could* like him. There never were two people more dissimilar. We have not one taste in common. We should be miserable' (348).

What Fanny is saying should not be missed. We have already encountered 'taste' used in conjunction with 'mind' and 'feeling', and this clear implication that 'taste' can provide an index of character is suggested in Johnson's *Dictionary* where it is glossed as 'perceptions, intellectual relish or discernment'. Yet Edmund shows himself deaf to any such implication, and he grossly misunderstands Fanny's words by associating morality with 'feelings' rather than 'principles':

> 'You are mistaken, Fanny. The dissimilarity is not so strong. You are quite enough alike. You *have* tastes in common. You have moral and literary tastes in

71

common. You have both warm hearts and benevolent feelings' (348).

Fanny is forced to begin again, more plainly:

'It is not merely in *temper* that I consider him as totally unsuited to myself . . . there is something in him which I object to still more. I must say, cousin, that I cannot approve his character. I have not thought well of him from the time of the play. I then saw him behaving, as it appeared to me, so very improperly and unfeelingly . . . so improperly by poor Mr. Rushworth, not seeming to care how he exposed or hurt him, and paying attentions to my cousin Maria, which – in short, at the time of the play, I received an impression which will never be got over' (349).

Edmund passes this off as 'that period of general folly', but Fanny has a keener sense where most blame should lie: 'Before the play, I am much mistaken, if *Julia* did not think he was paying her attentions' (350). In answer to this, Edmund seemingly forgets the conversation they have earlier had, and the extent of his lapse, not merely of memory but of judgment, is made clear when he says, 'There could be nothing very striking, because it is clear that he had no pretensions; his heart was reserved for you. And I must say, that its being for you, has raised him inconceivably in my opinion.' This does not merit a reply, and Fanny therefore tries to voice her objection in general terms: 'I am persuaded that he does not think as he ought, on serious subjects.' Edmund puts this down to Henry's having been led astray by his uncle, and suggests that Fanny, 'firm as a rock in her own principles' (351), will be the very woman to improve him. Understandably she shrinks from such a task, and Edmund, who admits he cannot be disinterested where Crawford is concerned, allows himself to run on about Mary and says how much she desires the match.

The conclusion of their talk allows Edmund to feel a reinforced confidence in his own view of the situation. Ironically, Fanny gives him grounds for this by using the last weapon in her armoury:

> 'He took me wholly by surprise. I had not an idea that his behaviour to me before had any meaning; and surely I was not to be teaching myself to like him only because he was taking, what seemed, very idle notice of me. In my situation, it would have been the extreme of vanity to be forming expectations on Mr. Crawford. . . . How then was I to be – to be in love with him the moment he said he was with me?' (353)

Fanny is here defending herself against the reported outrage of Henry's sisters, who think her out of her mind for refusing their brother. She is nevertheless right to doubt his taking, at first, serious notice of her, for the brutal ineptness of Henry's earlier words to Mary is not easily forgotten: 'I cannot be satisfied without Fanny Price, without making a small hole in Fanny Price's heart' (229). Her significant hesitation – which suggests, perhaps, how hard it is for her to put into words the mere idea of being in love with Henry – is totally lost on Edmund, who has proved himself throughout to be a bad listener. He not only misses the point she makes about the delicacy of human relationships and the complete lack on her part of any 'second feeling' towards Henry – that (in her words) 'it ought not to be set down as certain, that a man must be acceptable to every woman he may happen to like himself (353). He is also obviously deaf to the careful concession or qualification she begins with: 'But even supposing it is so, allowing Mr. Crawford to have all the claims which his sisters think he has. . . .'

Admittedly Fanny seems closer to thinking of Henry seriously while suffering the privations of Portsmouth than at any other time. Jane's brother Henry Austen, progressively reading the manuscript, admired Crawford (as the author herself said) 'properly, as a clever, pleasant man'. And a few days later she wrote,

> 'Henry has this moment said that he likes my M.P. better & better; he is in the 3d volume. I believe *now* he has changed his mind as to foreseeing the end; he said yesterday at least, that he defied anybody to say whether H.C. would be reformed, or would forget Fanny in a fortnight.'[6]

This is, nevertheless, one of the elements of the plot that Jane Austen handles with a kind of authorial double standard. On the one hand she implies that her heroine could not 'have escaped heart-whole from the courtship (though the courtship only of a fortnight) of such a man as Crawford . . . had not her affection been engaged elsewhere' (231). On the other hand she has Fanny's 'judgment' (324) reject Henry – and to have her heroine do otherwise, even at Portsmouth, where she thinks him 'altogether improved' (406), would have undermined the moral basis on which her character is constructed. In her final chapter Jane Austen states that had Henry 'persevered, and uprightly, Fanny must have been his reward' (467) – having earlier suggested that Fanny's opposition to him proceeds from her misplaced conviction that 'he never could have engaged' her 'affections': 'So thought Fanny in good truth and sober sadness' (329). Yet what Fanny feels for Henry at Portsmouth never proceeds beyond a limited kind of friendship. While she comes to notice 'a degree of friendliness – of interest at least – which was making his manner perfect' (400), her positively downright feelings are 'that he was and must ever be completely unsuited to her, and ought not to think of her' (405). Moreover, even at Portsmouth the reader is invited to notice that Henry continues to have a sense of the effect he is creating – almost to gauge his behaviour to suit his own intended advantage: 'He perceived that enough had been said of Everingham, and that it would be as well to talk of something else, and turned to Mansfield.'

In first speaking to Fanny of his love, Henry appeared not as 'the clandestine, insidious, treacherous admirer of Maria Bertram' but as 'the Mr. Crawford . . . addressing herself with ardent, disinterested, love; whose feelings were apparently become all that was honourable and upright, whose views of happiness were all fixed on a marriage of attachment' (327–8). This is what he 'apparently' was 'as far as words could prove it', and Fanny feels 'she must be courteous, and she must be compassionate'. But when he will not take her refusal for an answer, and still perseveres as confidently as before, she becomes 'angry': 'Here was again a want of delicacy and regard for others which had formerly so struck and disgusted her' (328–9) – or, to put it in stronger terms, 'a gross want of feeling and humanity where his own pleasure was concerned' (329). We are told that Fanny's 'manner was incurably gentle', and that this could be interpreted by someone like Crawford as 'almost an effort of self-denial' (327); as though he found something curiously teasing in Fanny's reluctance – just as he had found her manner so enigmatic that he had resolved he would make her like him: 'It was a love which, operating on an active, sanguine spirit, of more warmth than delicacy, made her affection appear of greater consequence, because it was withheld, and determined him to have the glory, as well as the felicity, of forcing her to love him' (326).

In seeking to come close to Fanny and draw her close to him, Henry may be seen to engage in a kind of parody of genuine intimacy by forcing his attentions on her and seeking to elicit her attentiveness in return. Even Sir Thomas discerns 'in a grand and careless way' that Henry is 'somewhat distinguishing his niece' (238), and a large portion of vanity marks his continuing attentions towards her. Mary, too, touches on a related point in describing Henry's courtship of Fanny when she alludes to him as 'quite the hero of an old romance' who 'glories in his chains' (360). Indeed, this same predisposition – reflecting a vanity sufficiently self-conscious – explains Henry's love of acting, almost his wish to make all the world his stage. During the episode of the earlier theatricals, Maria noticed that Henry's view was that 'the *performance*, not the *theatre*' ought to be their real 'object' (124), and it is not then merely Henry's flirting with Fanny, or even the figure he would want to cut as a preacher, which remains so characteristic of him. Rather it is also his sense that he could 'undertake any character that ever was written, from Shylock or Richard III. down to the singing hero of a farce' – that he 'could be any thing or every thing' (123).

Fanny can hear Henry read Shakespeare with a fascination that interrupts her work, and this serves to remind us of the power of the 'truly dramatic' (337). Even the otherwise inert Lady Bertram is moved to utter several sentences: 'You have a great turn for acting, I am sure, Mr. Crawford . . . I think you will have a theatre, some time or other, at your house in Norfolk' (338–9). But the vocabulary of acting has already become peculiarly sensitised because of its use in earlier contexts; in particular, the context it is given during the rehearsing of *Lovers' Vows* now reflects adversely on Henry. Fanny 'did not like him as a man, but she must admit him to be the best actor' (165). Julia, too, 'distrusted' his manoeuvring: 'He was, perhaps, but at treacherous play with her' (135). Edmund, so enamoured of Mary, fails to notice 'Julia's discomposure' because he is, as it were, no longer in real possession of himself, being 'between his theatrical and his real part, between Miss Crawford's claims and his own conduct, between love and consistency' (163). Such a passage gives a deliberate weighting to the 'real' and 'consistent' in an assessment of conduct, and a significance beyond embarrassed shyness to Fanny's protestations: 'I really cannot act' (146); 'I could not act any thing if you were to give me the world' (145). Acting, then, unless by 'hardened' (124) professionals, may be taken to reflect a felicity too easily shading into a facility, a something too much on the surface, almost an element of trick or contrivance – Henry, it will be remembered, was said to have 'the happiest knack, the happiest power of jumping and guessing' (337). It is as if the ability to enter so readily into a variety of parts and emotions were the sign of a character not sufficiently grounded in itself, so that there is nothing to prevent its indulgence in something else.[7] Interestingly, the Crawfords had only seemed to themselves 'all alive' (225) at the time of the play. Nor are we invited to discount the effect of such acting as a dangerous kind of wish-fulfilment. Maria and Henry both indulge their fantasies under cover of acting, and if Maria's is the more intense and lasting, Henry's also has unfortunate consequences for him.

In Henry vivacity and vanity seem thoroughly mingled. He imagines himself in the role of a 'distinguished preacher' (341), as needing an educated 'London audience . . . capable of estimating [his] composition'; but even this he would not like as 'a constancy', preferring instead to be 'anxiously expected for half a dozen Sundays together'. When Fanny involuntarily shakes her head, Henry presses to learn her meaning: '"Perhaps, Sir," said Fanny, wearied at last into speaking – "perhaps, Sir, I thought it was a pity you did not always know yourself as well as you seemed to do at that moment"' (343). This is a searing reproof, yet Henry seems altogether unabashed. He does, however, come to acknowledge that his future behaviour must speak for him:

'It is not by protestations that I shall endeavour to

convince you I am wronged, it is not by telling you that my affections are steady. My conduct shall speak for me – absence, distance, time shall speak for me. *They* shall prove, that as far as you can be deserved by any body, I do deserve you.'

Fanny always seems to know that she would never be able to share her thoughts and feelings with Henry Crawford. There is a weariness in her response to him – even in the politeness she shows him – that arguably reflects this. When he approaches her, the private space around her seems to collapse, so that she has a sense of being oppressed by him; and this (at its most acute) can seem 'a grievous imprisonment of body and mind' (344). Yet despite this, Fanny seems resigned to leave the proof of Henry to the future. At Portsmouth she listens to the account of his exertions at Everingham, and though she will not counsel him, she seems to accept his protestations at face value – 'to go back into Norfolk directly' (412) – even though his sister writes to say that Henry will be needed at Mrs Fraser's party on the 14th: 'Whether Mr. Crawford went into Norfolk before or after the 14th, was certainly no concern of her's, though, every thing considered, she thought he *would* go without delay' (418). When Edmund writes, he is able to tell her that he has seen Henry at Mrs Fraser's party: 'I am more and more satisfied with all that I see and hear of him. There is not a shadow of wavering. He thoroughly knows his own mind, and *acts up* to his resolutions' (423, my italics). The shock or horror of recognition comes with the use once again of this precise vocabulary. Henry has stayed in London with disastrous consequences. He has again met Maria and again been entangled by his vanity – though this time, it would appear, he has been entangled against his will.

Henry does finally 'act' on a very public stage, his 'audience' being not just London but all those who, like Fanny's father at Portsmouth, read of his doings in the press. It is through Mary's attempt to play these down, to dismiss this adulterous relationship with Maria as 'a moment's *etourderie*' (437), and to brazen it out as such to Edmund, that he eventually comes to see her more through Fanny's eyes. In his final interview with her, he tells her plainly how much his pain is increased by her seemingly light-hearted attempt to pass off what he can only regard as a 'sin' (458). As he leaves, she opens the door behind and calls after him, and her look and tone as she stands there, seeking to lure him again, are our most vivid reminder of what this particular Hercules has to turn his back on:

> '"Mr. Bertram," said she. I looked back. "Mr. Bertram," said she, with a smile – but it was a smile ill-suited to the conversation that had passed, a saucy playful smile, seeming to invite, in order to subdue me; at least, it appeared so to me. I resisted; it was the impulse of the moment to resist, and still walked on' (459).

When Fanny first learns of Henry and Maria, the shock she feels is very great. What 'her heart revolted from' is put in these terms:

> A woman married only six months ago, a man professing himself devoted, even *engaged*, to another – that other her near relation – the whole family, both families connected as they were by tie upon tie, all friends, all intimate together! – it was too horrible a confusion of guilt, too gross a complication of evil, for human nature, not in a state of utter barbarism, to be capable of! (441)

This exclamatory quality in some sense extends to the novel itself, at least in terms of the moral values it seeks to endorse. Trilling observes that *Mansfield Park* has an obviously 'metaphysical' dimension;[8] in a way uncharacteristic of the other novels, it appeals to abstract concepts rather than negotiates subtle judgments in the give-and-take of social and personal relationships. For this reason, despite the power of individual scenes, it fails adequately to dramatise or internalise what it seeks to hold in solution. The result is, in fact, a kind of dissociation of sensibility – 'a book divided against itself'[9] – in the way virtue and vice are juxtaposed (the debate in the chapel at Sotherton between Edmund and Mary being conducted in these terms).

In the words of Julia Brown, 'the real crisis of the novel has to do with an interior failure – the failure of the individual human spirit to renew itself.'[10] For all that Jane Austen implies of her brother's reaction in reading it, and for all that she herself writes in the closing chapter, *Mansfield Park* presents a closing off of human possibilities. Not only are offenders (like the Crawfords) unhesitatingly damned, but those moments when moral perception and imaginative power are vividly interfused – like the episode of Fanny dressing for the ball, where she weighs and seemingly resolves the 'claims' (271) being made upon her – are not developed in an integrated way within the externalised claims of the action. Even in the final pages of the novel, scant allowance is made for Fanny's presence as a person. Our final impression is that a lack of genuine human responsiveness remains characteristic of Mansfield. Sir Thomas has a sense of 'rearing' for himself 'a prime comfort' (472), while Edmund has a sense of her being 'only too good for him' (471). John Bayley has noted 'the arbitrary winding-up of the plot' in these terms: 'Fanny's triumphant marriage is not earned nor even indulged by anything crucial in the presentation of her.'[11]

Though Fanny speaks of the major characters as 'all intimate together', it is the way they are kept apart that virtually guarantees the overall impression of disjunction.

Even when Edmund, after becoming disillusioned about Mary, continues to talk of her, the terms in which he does so are merely his attempt to create the grounds for a factitious kind of intimacy: '. . . how she had attached him, and how delightful nature had made her, and how excellent she would have been . . .' (459). Fanny is obliged to open his eyes to Mary 'by some hint of what share his brother's state of health might be supposed to have in her wish for a complete reconciliation'. Concerning the date of Edmund's subsequent attachment to Fanny, the author has therefore to be rather coy:

> I only intreat every body to believe that exactly at the time when it was quite natural that it should be so, and not a week earlier, Edmund did cease to care about Miss Crawford, and became as anxious to marry Fanny, as Fanny herself could desire (470).

While Jane Austen not insignificantly notes what we have somehow been conscious of all along – that Fanny was to Edmund 'an object . . . of such close and peculiar interest' (470) – the reader is virtually left to infer how this 'close and peculiar interest' will ensure their future happiness.

Emma Woodhouse

Despite Jane Austen's suggestion that in writing *Emma* she
was creating a heroine whom no one but herself would
'much like',[1] 'there is', to adapt Mr Knightley's words, 'an
anxiety, a curiosity in what one feels for Emma' (40).
While such a remark indicates Knightley's interest in her as
a person, an interest he comes later to realise as love, our
interest as readers is captured by a vitality so immediate
that even in its waywardness it compels our fascinated
participation. John Bayley has aptly described 'the whole
tendency of the novel' in terms of its 'enveloping
intimacy',[2] and this proceeds from a quality of imagination evident in the very first sentence:

> Emma Woodhouse, handsome, clever, and rich, with a
> comfortable home and happy disposition, seemed to
> unite some of the best blessings of existence; and had
> lived nearly twenty-one years in the world with very
> little to distress or vex her (5).

The creation of Emma and her world is as seamless as this
blending of the heroine's consciousness and the author's. It
appears that Emma seems to herself what is being said of
her, her happiness being as conscious as it seems to her
unalloyed. She is conscious of having almost come of age,
and therefore of being (what she has really never doubted,
though always attentive to her father) at her own disposal
– almost of having herself to thank for being 'the fair

mistress of the mansion' (22). The irony of her having had 'very little to distress or vex her' is therefore lost on her, even though it is, as irony, sufficiently indulgent. It anticipates the kind of point almost immediately given it, and subsequently reinforced by later episodes.

Emma is so positive about having 'made the match' (11) between Miss Taylor and Mr Weston that the reader naturally inclines to Knightley's bluff scepticism: 'A straight-forward, open-hearted man, like Weston, and a rational unaffected woman, like Miss Taylor, may be safely left to manage their own concerns' (13). We soon learn that Weston had, over a long period, intended to secure a 'little estate adjoining Highbury' (16). Apparently he had also for some considerable period intended marrying Miss Taylor:

> It was now some time since Miss Taylor had begun to influence his schemes. . . . He had made his fortune, bought his house, and obtained his wife; and was beginning a new period of existence with every probability of greater happiness than in any yet passed through (16–17).

If this is a somewhat phlegmatic manner of proceeding, it may be counted in Emma's favour that her wish outran the event. But this tendency in her also has its dangerous side, as Knightley is quick to point out: 'You are more likely to have done harm to yourself, than good to them, by interference' (13).

Emma is so concerned to direct her energies at will that for much of the novel this prevents Knightley from sharing anything approaching intimacy with her. It is true that they know each other well, that she playfully responds to his presence, and that he finds her tantalising. But he is also prepared to be frank with her even though she is wilful enough not to want to listen. She must therefore be prepared to laugh off what he says, to treat it (in her own words) as 'all a joke'; and she revealingly adds, 'We always say what we like to one another' (10).

This argues that a special kind of relationship exists between them, beyond what is implied by his being her brother-in-law. If they can use this degree of freedom, without rudeness, to each other, then there is an almost unconscious basis for a further and different kind of sharing. Yet Emma is still a long way from realising this, even though in missing Mrs Weston as her companion she is at a loss for someone who can fill a comparable place in her affection. That the potential of what passes between Knightley and herself only comes, much later, to be acknowledged for what it is means that Emma is virtually bound to become involved with Harriet Smith. Her friend's claims exist, however, only in her imaginaton. While Emma allows Harriet's being 'so artlessly impressed by the appearance of every thing in so superior a style' to make up for her lack of cleverness, and even to argue her 'good sense' (23), Knightley is in no doubt that what has been developing between the two young women is 'a very foolish intimacy' (64). But his words are wasted on Emma, who becomes involved in an absorbing kind of game to which she devotes all her boundless energy and enthusiasm.

Harriet's head is soon turned by her being persuaded to think of the clergyman Mr Elton, and Emma is instrumental in having her refuse an offer of marriage from her old sweetheart Robert Martin. This nettles Knightley, who has a justifiable regard for Martin, and he presses Emma so closely on the matter that she is even forced to prevaricate with him about her part in it all. Yet her confidence is shaken no longer than it takes her to provide herself with reassurance, and immediate events seem to favour her, for Harriet returns with news that Elton has been seen riding to London on a 'very enviable commission' as 'the bearer of something exceedingly precious' (68) – the portrait that Emma has drawn of Harriet.

The humour of this episode is enlivened by the exuberance with which Emma continually misunderstands the would-be suitor's intentions. When she admits to her former 'great passion for taking likenesses', Elton becomes quite rhapsodic:

'Let me entreat you, Miss Woodhouse, to exercise so charming a talent in favour of your friend. I know what your drawings are. How could you suppose me ignorant? Is not this room rich in specimens of your landscapes and flowers; and has not Mrs. Weston some inimitable figure-pieces in her drawing-room, at Randalls?' (43)

Such veiled flattery could never, of course, capture Emma's interest even if her head were not full of other plans. As it is, she entirely misses the drift of what Elton is saying: 'Yes, good man! – thought Emma – but what has all that to do with taking likenesses? You know nothing of drawing. Don't pretend to be in raptures about mine. Keep your raptures for Harriet's face' (43). She ridiculously wills Elton to embrace her own view of his affections, and is not beyond giving to Harriet's portrait a few improving touches. Though we may accuse her of partiality, and even of blindness, we respond to her enthusiasm not only because it is so well intentioned, but also because it is so deliciously misplaced.

Emma's failure to discern Elton's intentions becomes even more obvious during the episode of charades – a failure all the more ludicrous because of her consciousness of her own sagacity. Indeed Emma becomes for herself the measure of all things – even to the extent of a presumed rewriting of Shakespeare. She supposes that any Hartfield edition would need a long note on the line, 'The course of true love never did run smooth.' There are, moreover, no lengths she is unwilling to go in furthering her scheme for Harriet. On their return from a 'charitable visit' (83) just outside Highbury, Elton joins them in their walk, and Emma is concerned to fall a little behind in order to leave him and Harriet together. Yet when she cannot help but rejoin them, she finds Elton's 'animation' has been expended only on 'giving his fair companion an account of the yesterday's party at his friend Cole's, and that she was come in herself for the Stilton cheese, the north Wiltshire, the butter, the cellery, the beet-root and all the dessert' (88–9). Emma tries to console herself with the important truism that 'any thing interests between those who love'; yet the thought seems ridiculous when applied to this conversation between Elton and Harriet. Its potential application to Knightley and herself seems, however, entirely lost on Emma.

When the plain-speaking John Knightley arrives on the scene, Emma is amused at his idea of Elton's being in love with her, at least to the extent that it allows her to reflect on 'the mistakes which people of high pretensions to judgment are for ever falling into'. (112) And when Harriet becomes ill with an ulcerated throat, and Elton seems more anxious that Emma should not catch the infection, she becomes 'vexed' (125) – an experience, we remember, it had not previously been her lot much to suffer. Her first real nemesis occurs, however, when Elton proposes to her in the carriage on the way home from Randalls. She reflects on his 'presumption' (130) even though she herself has been so strongly expecting him to form an 'attachment' (131) to Harriet, 'the natural daughter of somebody', (22). And when at last Emma can seek 'the relief of quiet reflection' (133), she begins by expressing disappointment for her own cherished scheme. Though she also feels the bitter disappointment for Harriet, it is a moot point how contrite she for her part is feeling. Indeed, it at first seems that she is distressed at the thwarting of her plans rather than at her own conduct in the affair:

> The hair was curled, and the maid sent away, and Emma sat down to think and be miserable. – It was a wretched business, indeed! – Such an overthrow of every thing she had been wishing for! – Such a development of every thing most unwelcome! – Such a blow for Harriet! – That was the worst of all. Every part of it brought pain and humiliation, of some sort or other; but, compared with the evil to Harriet, all was light; and she would gladly have submitted to feel yet more mistaken – more in error – more disgraced by mis-judgment, than she actually was, could the effects of her blunders have been confined to herself (134).

As Emma continues to reflect on Elton's proposal, she comes closer to admitting her own 'mis-judgment' – only to conclude that the blame for it must lie elsewhere: 'She had taken up the idea, she supposed, and made every thing bend to it. His manners, however, must have been unmarked, wavering, dubious, or she could not have been so misled.' That the Knightleys had seen more than herself causes her to blush: 'It was dreadfully mortifying' (135). 'You have been no friend to Harriet Smith, Emma' (63), Mr Knightley had said, and his remark is (however unconsciously) echoed in her admission to herself: 'I have been but half a friend to her' (137). Gradually she comes to look more leniently on Elton's mistake, acknowledging that there were some grounds for his 'conceited head' (136) to be so turned; and while she excuses him rather than implicates herself in any kind of conceit, she does nevertheless catch herself out in the very act of imagining an alternative suitor for Harriet.

Unlike the prosy and unpretentious Miss Bates, whose loquacity does not presume on what she does not know, Emma refuses to confine her busy imagination to what is

before her.[3] Yet it is not only her judgment but her sense
of common justice that is called into question when she
indulges her fancy about Jane Fairfax and the Mr Dixon
who has recently married Jane's friend. Miss Bates, so
genuinely grateful for other people's kindness to herself
and her mother, seemingly gets her stimulation from her
own incessant chatter. But the exercise of Emma's fancy
seems linked with her isolation, almost with some
thwarting on her part of her native intelligence through
her need to create some immediate object of interest. She
has not otherwise stored her mind, and we have been
alerted to the fact by Knightley's, 'I have done with
expecting any course of steady reading from Emma' (37).
Her fertile fancy therefore leads her into a kind of
unwarranted 'interference' in the concerns of others,
though the reader tends not to be alienated by this because
of her natural exuberance and unselfishness.

What has been called Emma's 'pleasurable ease of
imaginative activity'[4] is a delighted devotion to her own
imaginings, and to this extent these are intimately a part of
her inner vitality. As Miss Bates talks of Jane's friends, 'an
ingenious and animating suspicion entering Emma's brain'
(160), she is all too ready to put her own construction on
what she is told. Yet what she proceeds to accuse Jane of
soon becomes her reason for pitying her, since her own
romantic feelings (containing a hint even of the melo-
dramatic) allow her to picture to herself the possibility of
Jane's 'simple, single, successless love': 'She might have
been unconsciously sucking in the sad poison, while a
sharer of his conversation with her friend' (168). But when
Jane will not be unreserved with her, Emma's suspicions
return: 'Her caution was thrown away. Emma saw its
artifice, and returned to her first surmises' (169).

Emma's penchant for holding to these is nicely though
silently illustrated when, on a visit to Hartfield, Jane and
her aunt discuss Mr Dixon:

'Mr. Dixon, you say, is not, strictly speaking, hand-some.'

'Handsome! Oh! no – far from it – certainly plain. I told you he was plain.'

'My dear, you said that Miss Campbell would not allow him to be plain, and that you yourself – '

'Oh! as for me, my judgment is worth nothing. Where I have a regard, I always think a person well-looking. But I gave what I believed the general opinion, when I called him plain' (176).

Given the reserve Emma has noticed, it would be inconceivable to have Jane speak like this if her feelings were really engaged. Yet we sense that Emma is busily taking from the words whatever will feed her fancy – that it is Jane's regard for Mr Dixon which makes him seem handsome to her, or (not very consistently) that he really is handsome even though Jane protests his plainness in the eyes of the world.

When Emma, with an air of expectancy on her side, meets Frank Churchill, she has her mind made up about Jane and Mr Dixon; and her suspicions are soon reinforced by Frank's account of the gentleman's preferring Jane's playing to his fiancée's. This is an example to touch Emma's self-esteem since she has always been conscious of Jane's 'own very superior performance' (169). Perhaps, then, there is a peculiar satisfaction for her in allowing her brain to be so active on the subject. Though Frank points out that Jane was Miss Campbell's 'very particular friend', Emma laughingly says:

'Poor comfort! . . . One would rather have a stranger preferred than one's very particular friend – with a stranger it might not recur again – but the misery of having a very particular friend always at hand, to do every thing better than one does oneself! – Poor Mrs.

Dixon! Well, I am glad she is gone to settle in Ireland' (202).

During the dinner party at the Coles', Emma, hearing of the gift of a piano, reveals her suspicions to Frank. The animation she displays in indulging her flight of fancy has its counterpart in Frank's lively temper as he conducts a cat-and-mouse game in playing along with her whim:

'If Col. Campbell is not the person, who can be?'
  'What do you say to Mrs. Dixon?'
  'Mrs. Dixon! very true indeed. I had not thought of Mrs. Dixon. She must know as well as her father, how acceptable an instrument would be; and perhaps the mode of it, the mystery, the surprize, is more like a young woman's scheme than an elderly man's. It is Mrs. Dixon I dare say. I told you that your suspicions would guide mine.'
    'If so, you must extend your suspicions and compre-hend *Mr.* Dixon in them.'
  'Mr. Dixon. – Very well. Yes, I immediately perceive that it must be the joint present of Mr. and Mrs. Dixon. We were speaking the other day, you know, of his being so warm an admirer of her performance' (216–17).

Frank has seemingly not quite, even yet, penetrated to her full meaning, so that Emma is forced to be more explicit. Her suggestion is ungenerous and even indelicate, and she comes not only to doubt whether it does not transgress 'the duty of woman by woman' (231), but also to regret 'every former ungenerous suspicion' (380). Yet our sense of this is here obscured by Emma's zest for the idea she has conjured up – almost as though we take at face value her wish not to be judgmental:

'I do not mean to reflect upon the good intentions of either Mr. Dixon or Miss Fairfax, but I cannot help suspecting either that, after making his proposals to her

90

friend, he had the misfortune to fall in love with *her*, or that he became conscious of a little attachment on her side. One might guess twenty things without guessing exactly the right; but I am sure there must be a particular cause for her chusing to come to Highbury instead of going with the Campbells to Ireland' (217).

Though Emma finds Frank an animating presence, 'her feeling for him is no more than the lively notice that an attractive and vivacious girl takes of an attractive and vivacious young man.'[5] Nevertheless, her interest in him is at this stage decided enough to enable him to calculate his effect on her. Step by step he allows himself to seem drawn in to share her 'suspicions'. He admits 'they have an air of great probability', and his representing himself as plain and unseeing, after she has brought forward the near boating-accident, gives a fillip to her vanity even as he acknowledges, tongue-in-cheek, how little she needs it:

'If I had been there, I think I should have made some discoveries.'
   'I dare say you would; but I, simple I, saw nothing but the fact, that Miss Fairfax was nearly dashed from the vessel and that Mr. Dixon caught her. – It was the work of a moment. . . . I do not mean to say, however, that you might not have made discoveries' (218).

Encouraged and not seeing his irony, Emma can be more 'decisive' still, and when Frank further leads her on, she becomes quite positive, her earlier 'suspicions' reaching to a certainty: 'No, I am sure it is not from the Campbells. . . . I may not have convinced you perhaps, but I am perfectly convinced myself that Mr. Dixon is a principal in the business.' With an air of mock-innocence – and some violence to language – Frank acquiesces: 'Indeed you injure me if you suppose me unconvinced. Your reasonings carry my judgment along with them entirely' (218–9).

Under cover of talking about Jane and Mr Dixon, Emma plays up to the effect she thinks she is having on Frank. Her idea about Jane and her consciousness of him seem complementary satisfactions: 'There was no occasion to press the matter farther. The conviction seemed real; he looked as if he felt it' (219). She senses other people, the Westons particularly, are in imagination linking Frank and herself, and she is from the first willing to entertain the thought:

> He was a *very* good looking young man; height, air, address, all were unexceptionable . . . he looked quick and sensible. She felt immediately that she should like him; and there was a well-bred ease of manner, and a readiness to talk, which convinced her that he came intending to be acquainted with her, and that acquainted they soon must be (190).

Emma is quite unusually concerned to take Frank's measure as a person, and only his whim of going to London, ostensibly to get his hair cut, makes her at all baulk at the role she has pictured for him:

> But for such an unfortunate fancy for having his hair cut, there was nothing to denote him unworthy of the distinguished honour which her imagination had given him; the honour, if not of being really in love with her, of being at least very near it, and saved only by her own indifference – (for still her resolution held of never marrying) – the honour, in short, of being marked out for her by all their joint acquaintance (206).

There is a curious drawing-back here, mixed, perhaps, with a touch of imperiousness. Her interest in his presence is nevertheless very strong, and on his return from London, 'as undaunted and as lively as ever', Emma – again with some violence to language – 'thus moralized to herself':

'I do not know whether it ought to be so, but certainly
silly things do cease to be silly if they are done by sensible
people in an impudent way. Wickedness is always
wickedness, but folly is not always folly. – It depends
upon the character of those who handle it' (212).

'All their joint acquaintance' do not, however, see the
hidden motives of what passes between Frank and Emma.
He is pleased to admit her suspicions because they provide
a convenient cover for his own secret engagement to Jane;
and there is an element of another sort of 'trifling' – the
word Knightley uses to himself in a general sense, and
Emma picks up only to dismiss (206, 212). Jane can see
what Frank is doing in permitting himself to appear so
attentive and high-spirited towards Emma; and evidence
of how his behaviour is construed by others is provided by
Knightley's attempt to warn Emma, and by the Westons'
later concern for her feelings on hearing of the engagement. There is, too, Emma's own willingness to entertain
the idea that he should be in love with her. The supposed
romantic attachment between Jane and Mr Dixon gives to
the consciousness of her continuing by-play with Frank
the heightened colouring of enchanted ground.

Though Emma is willing to be flirted with and Frank
willing to seem to flirt with her, their words are never
such as to draw them closer together except in a quasi-
conspiratorial sense. When she visits the Bateses to hear
the new instrument, the kind of *double entendre* he indulges
in delights her even as she seems to feel it to be too
'pointed'. But when she sees that, despite Jane's 'deep
blush of consciousness, there had been a smile of secret
delight' (at Frank's reference to the 'new set of Irish
melodies' that accompanied the gift), Emma has 'much
less compunction with respect to her', almost a feeling of
moral superiority over the woman she has viewed as a
rival, and therefore never been able to like: 'This amiable,

upright, perfect Jane Fairfax was apparently cherishing very reprehensible feelings' (242, 243). Emma is certainly not blameless and yet she is herself the unwitting victim of the mutual confidence between Frank and Jane. The irony works against her even as she thinks it should be laying siege to Jane. Her continuing inability to get quite clear what she ought to feel should perhaps be regarded as a tacit sign of her uneasy part in the complicated game Frank Churchill is playing.

When Frank comes close to telling her about Jane ('Miss Woodhouse – I think you can hardly be quite without suspicion', 260), Emma jumps to the conclusion that he must be in love with her. As she thinks this over after his departure, she is unsure how much she is in love, though we are given a strong hint that her state of mind is clearly somewhere on this side of love by the kind of fanciful indulgence she goes in for:

> As she sat drawing or working, forming a thousand amusing schemes for the progress and close of their attachment, fancying interesting dialogues, and inventing elegant letters; the conclusion of every imaginary declaration on his side was that she *refused him* (264).

This provides a good example of how intimately we see Emma. We sense her enjoyment – without wishing to feel committed herself – in entertaining the possibility of Frank's being, after all, interested in Harriet:

> 'I know the danger of indulging such speculations. But stranger things have happened; and when we cease to care for each other as we do now, it will be the means of confirming us in that sort of true disinterested friendship which I can already look forward to with pleasure' (267).

There is a sense in which Emma lives vicariously and seems content to do so. In contemplating, for example, her future happiness in relation to her sister's children, she supposes that 'there will be enough of them . . . to supply every sort of sensation that declining life can need' (86). This same tendency allows her to regard people and events as 'interesting' – like 'the interesting day' of Frank Churchill's arrival (189) – without committing herself to them beyond a certain imaginative indulgence. In fact, her being such an 'imaginist' implies her ability to be 'on fire with speculation' (335) without forgoing her curious kind of self-dramatisation or uninvolvement. She can, as Mrs Weston notices, 'get upon delicate subjects' (201) precisely because she has so little of her real emotional self invested in them. When Emma knows she is not in love with Frank (at first a person 'so high in interest', 190), she tends to imagine that his 'restlessness' and 'agitated spirits' proceed from his 'dread of her returning power' (316). After he has arrived hot and bothered at the Donwell strawberry-picking, she smiles 'her acceptance' (366) that he should join them next day in their outing to Box Hill. At Box Hill, where Frank, to begin with, is 'dull' and 'silent' (367) and Emma feels 'less happy than she had expected' (368), they both enter into a degree of flirtatiousness that she for her part had not experienced at the ball (326). It is as though each tries to draw the interest of the other, and in their frustration they engage in a fooling that oversteps the bounds of social acceptability[6] and touches suggestive areas for the very consciousness of doing so:

'It is hotter to-day.'
'Not to my feelings. I am perfectly comfortable to-day.'
'You are comfortable because you are under command.'
'Your command? – Yes.'
'Perhaps I intended you to say so, but I meant self-command . . . as I cannot be always with you, it is best

to believe your temper under your own command
rather than mine.'

'It comes to the same thing. I can have no self–
command without a motive. You order me, whether
you speak or not. And you can be always with me. You
are always with me' (368–9).

Linked together in this way without ever being close, they
try to rouse the others to some show of animation,
proposing that everyone should say 'one thing very
clever . • . or two things moderately clever – or three
things very dull indeed' (370). When Miss Bates volun-
teers herself for the last category, Emma cannot 'resist' a
quip at her expense. Here the disregard of others that has
marked her fooling with Frank issues in an unpardonable
rudeness to an 'old friend' (371) of her family: 'Ah! ma'am,
but there may be a difficulty. Pardon me – but you will be
limited as to number – only three at once' (370).

If Box Hill shows Emma giving herself up to the heated
extravagance of an over-indulged imagination, what
evidence do we have that there is another side to her
personality and feelings? There is, most immediately, the
contrition she feels at Knightley's rebuke when he has
proved himself her 'friend by very faithful counsel' (375).
There is, too, her constant attentiveness to her valetudi-
narian father; indeed, 'as a daughter, she hoped she was
not without a heart': 'She hoped no one could have said to
her, "How could you be so unfeeling to your father?"'
(377). The use of 'heart' here signals the deeper reality. She
has felt Knightley's rebuke 'at her heart' (376), and the
recognition this implies is itself a corrective to that earlier
attitude when, pleased by Harriet's 'gratitude', she had
exclaimed to herself, 'There is no charm equal to tenderness of heart' (269). Given the moral tradition Jane Austen
shared with Dr Johnson, this remark seems bound to call
down a moral judgment upon Emma. Despite what she

says in her own defence about her rudeness to Miss Bates, she is obliged to learn that there is a virtue in what she had opposed to 'tenderness of heart', namely, 'clearness of head'. She is obliged to learn that virtue as something solid and substantial depends on how we actually behave towards others. Significantly she laments 'the blindness of her own head and heart' (411–12) when forced to contemplate Harriet and Knightley. It has already 'darted through her, with the speed of an arrow, that Mr. Knightley must marry no one but herself' (408), and the suggestiveness of this image is enhanced when we remember that Cupid's arrows traditionally entered through the eye (or head) to lodge in the heart.

When Emma comes to know her love for Knightley, she also comes to know herself. Elton's proposal had shaken her confidence in her own perspicacity, but it had not led her to abandon her propensity for match-making, or her 'interference' in the concerns of others; it had only led her to be more circumspect in voicing to Harriet her hopes for her. Emma's mistaken notions about Jane also affect her deeply. On first hearing news of the secret engagement with Frank, 'her mind was divided between two ideas – her own former conversations with him about Miss Fairfax; and poor Harriet' (395), whom she has been silently encouraging in what she imagines is her secret love for Frank. A little later in her conversation with Mrs Weston, she thinks Jane and Frank's 'a very abominable sort of proceeding':

'What has it been but a system of hypocrisy and deceit, – espionage, and treachery? – To come among us with professions of openness and simplicity; and such a league in secret to judge us all! – Here have we been, the whole winter and spring, completely duped' (399).

Frank and Jane cannot be exonerated; yet the strength of Emma's language appears more than a trifle defensive.

Reflection, however, convinces her that her own suspicions were 'abominable' (421), and that these 'she had
not only so foolishly fashioned and harboured herself, but
had so unpardonably imparted' (421).

To give even this account of Emma's progress towards
self-knowledge, is, however, to overlook not only the
peculiarly complex way in which Jane and Harriet mingle
in her thoughts, but the reason for the prominence she
gives them – Emma's interest in Harriet having essentially
stemmed from her inability to recognise her latent feeling
for Knightley. While so much of the novel unfolds, as it
were, through Emma's consciousness, the conflicting
claims of Harriet and Jane are not therefore easily
objectified. Justice to Harriet can be used as a reason for
putting thoughts of Jane aside; but when the situation of
Harriet seems to alter, Emma can reproach herself for not
having made more of Jane:

> Had she followed Mr. Knightley's known wishes, in
> paying that attention to Miss Fairfax, which was every
> way her due; had she tried to know her better; had she
> done her part towards intimacy; had she endeavoured to
> find a friend there instead of in Harriet Smith; she must,
> in all probability, have been spared from every pain
> which pressed on her now (421).

The accomplished Jane has seemed too much like a rival
whereas Harriet has been Emma's protégé:

> As far as her mind could disengage itself from the
> injustice and selfishness of angry feelings, she acknowl-
> edged that Jane Fairfax would have neither elevation nor
> happiness beyond her desert. But poor Harriet was such
> an engrossing charge! There was little sympathy to be
> spared for any body else (403).

Emma now acknowledges the full force of what she seems
unconsciously to have only half acknowledged before:

'Mr. Knightley had spoken prophetically, when he once said, "Emma, you have been no friend to Harriet Smith"' (402). But when she learns that Harriet has never thought of Frank, and has her thoughts fixed on Knightley, Emma is in a state of 'consternation' (407). She is silenced by Harriet's disclaimer about Frank ('Him! – never, never', 405), and waits 'in great terror' for her to name Knightley. Again she is beforehand with her guess, though this time, when she would have it otherwise, she guesses correctly.

This episode gives a further opportunity for Emma to appraise 'her own conduct', and here, as it were for the first time in the novel, her own feelings are inescapably involved in the situation:

> She saw it all with a clearness which had never blessed her before. How improperly had she been acting by Harriet! How inconsiderate, how indelicate, how irrational, how unfeeling had been her conduct! What blindness, what madness, had led her on! It struck her with dreadful force, and she was ready to give it every bad name in the world (408).

To take this as wholly straight is to miss something, for Emma is claiming to see with 'clearness' while using the term 'improperly' in a sense that cannot be entirely disinterested: she is 'struck . . . with dreadful force' not just by her former conduct but by the overthrow of her own personal wishes; and there is the heightened language ('every bad name in the world') which in fact emphasises her degree of involvement. Not surprisingly then, when Harriet finally leaves her, she bursts out with, 'Oh God! that I had never seen her' (411).

Emma becomes more clear-sighted about her feelings, even though it takes Harriet's revelation to force her to acknowledge them. She now asks herself when Mr Knightley had supplanted Frank Churchill in her affections. As she compares the two, she comes to realise what she had so long allowed herself to be blind to:

> She saw that there never had been a time when she did not consider Mr. Knightley as infinitely the superior, or when his regard for her had not been infinitely the most dear. She saw, that in persuading herself, in fancying, in acting to the contrary, she had been entirely under a delusion, totally ignorant of her own heart – and, in short, that she had never really cared for Frank Churchill at all! (412).

The exclamatory quality of this is amusing, yet it expresses the essential truth. A little later, when a solicitous Knightley tries to comfort her for the loss of Frank, Emma can assure him that her feelings were not engaged. She is 'ashamed' that her 'manners gave such an impression' (426), and she has 'very little to say' for her conduct:

> 'I was tempted by his attentions, and allowed myself to appear pleased. – An old story, probably – a common case – and no more than has happened to hundreds of my sex before; and yet it may not be the more excusable in one who sets up as I do for Understanding' (427).

She can think of reasons why she was tempted, but she also confesses that they all 'centre' in this: 'My vanity was flattered, and I allowed his attentions.'

This is Emma acknowledging without any equivocation or accompanying irony the very thing Knightley had said to Mrs Weston. In praising her for not being 'personally vain', he had added, 'Her vanity lies another way' (39). Building on her recent admission to herself of 'the blindness of her own head and heart', she is now seeing herself with a clarity that has never been hers before. There seems a related significance both in the change in the weather ('the wind changed into a softer quarter; the clouds were carried off; the sun appeared; it was summer again', 424), and in the fact that Knightley is now with her. He is still to speak his feelings, but it seems significant that she should have acknowledged this before he does. It signals her growth in self-knowledge, and with it her maturity as a woman.

Since Knightley comes to Hartfield as soon as the novel opens, the reader who has been aware not only of his constant attentiveness to Emma and her concerns, but also of the false note that is struck in her conversations with Frank Churchill, will be inclined to ignore the false lead of the younger man. The Oxford editor of the novels has noticed those occasions when 'Mr. Knightley comes unbidden, and sometimes unrecognized, into Emma's thoughts'.[7] She thinks to herself, after the ball has apparently been called off, that 'Mr. Knightley will be happy' (262). She condemns Frank's dissimulation by standards that can only be drawn from knowledge of another, very different kind of man (397). And she has the consolation of knowing Knightley would have approved had he 'been privy to all her attempts of assisting Jane Fairfax' (391). But arguably the most revealing aspect of what she is forced to acknowledge concerns her sense of Mr Weston's merely 'general friendship' (320). In going early to the ball in response to his particular and earnest 'entreaties', Emma is disconcerted at finding herself among so many other 'intimates and confidantes'. Almost involuntarily, as it were, she measures off such behaviour against what she knows of another, with an almost explicit recognition of the importance of a very different kind of bearing: 'General benevolence, but not general friendship, made a man what he ought to be. – She could fancy such a man.' This recognition is soon reinforced during the outing to Donwell by the consciousness Emma has of its owner. As her eye ranges from the house to its 'ample gardens' and 'meadows', taking in the avenues of trees, it is especially the character of Knightley which seems so present to her (358). As in Ben Jonson's 'To Penhurst', nothing is here of 'envious show'; and yet in the unspoilt nature that greets the eye and carries into the heart, Emma implicitly recognises that here too its owner 'dwells'.[8]

This is not articulated in precisely these terms; indeed, Emma's 'pleasant feelings' are rather too much aware of the Donwell family's impeccable origins. But Donwell at least gives her time to reflect on something unspoilt and substantial – until, that is, she is forced to join the others around the strawberry beds, where Mrs Elton, herself totally lacking in inner resources, talks herself to a standstill without deriving any real enjoyment from what is before her. Elsewhere there is more than one indication that when Emma can be both relaxed and spontaneous she shows something of her inner self. Of course, there are many times when Knightley tries to talk seriously to her and she, for one reason or another, is concerned to oppose him. Even the first chapter contains an instance of her defensiveness, and their conversation about Harriet, Frank or Jane provide others. But there are those other times when something very different happens, when wit and good humour and a heartfelt exuberance all seem to combine.

An example is what passes between Knightley and herself on their arrival at the Coles'. Emma compliments him on having come in his carriage: 'This is coming as you should do . . . like a gentleman. – I am quite glad to see you' (213). As he tries to pass this off with, 'If we had met first in the drawing-room, I doubt whether you would have discerned me to be more of a gentleman than usual', Emma defends herself in these terms:

'Yes I should, I am sure I should. There is always a look of consciousness or bustle when people come in a way which they know to be beneath them. You think you carry it off very well, I dare say, but with you it is a sort of bravado, an air of affected unconcern; I always observe it whenever I meet you under those circumstances. *Now* you have nothing to try for. You are not afraid of being supposed ashamed. You are not striving to look taller than any body else. *Now* I shall really be very happy to walk into the same room with you' (213–14).

Emma doubtless begins as she does because of her uncertainty about the propriety of accepting this particular invitation. Excessive consciousness of her position is one of the traits she only progressively loses throughout the novel. She is therefore particularly mindful of what is appropriate to 'the owner of Donwell Abbey' (213) – whereas Knightley would have used his carriage for an entirely different reason, to seem not to slight his hosts, who might anyway have been feeling somewhat diffident (though his other reason was, of course, to make his carriage available to Miss Bates and her niece). As Emma continues, however, her words come to have a suggestion of warmth that draws Knightley and herself closer. She playfully and naturally pictures them as walking in together. His reaction, though characteristically brief, is affectionate, and seems to acknowledge all that Emma has been saying: '"Nonsensical girl!" was his reply, but not at all in anger' (214).

Another example of wit and natural ease, spontaneous and affectionate good humour, occurs at the end of the second volume; and its being placed there gives us an anticipation of what is to come in the final volume. John Knightley, who has left his little boys in Emma's care, suggests that if they prove to be in the way of her increased social life she must send them home.

'No,' cried Mr. Knightley, 'that need not be the

consequence. Let them be sent to Donwell. I shall
certainly be at leisure.'

'Upon my word,' exclaimed Emma, 'you amuse me!
I should like to know how many of all my numerous
engagements take place without your being of the party;
and why I am to be supposed in danger of wanting
leisure to attend to the little boys. These amazing
engagements of mine – what have they been? Dining
once with the Coles – and having a ball talked of, which
never took place. I can understand you – (nodding at
Mr. John Knightley) – your good fortune in meeting
with so many of your friends at once here, delights you
too much to pass unnoticed. But you, (turning to Mr.
Knightley,) who know how very, very seldom I am
ever two hours from Hartfield, why you should foresee
such a series of dissipation for me, I cannot imagine.
And as to my dear little boys, I must say, that if aunt
Emma has not time for them, I do not think they would
fare much better with uncle Knightley, who is absent
from home about five hours where she is absent one –
and who, when he is at home, is either reading to
himself or settling his accounts.'

Mr. Knightley seemed to be trying not to smile; and
succeeded without difficulty, upon Mrs. Elton's beginning to talk to him (312).

This scene suggests what provides a sure foundation for
the romance of Emma and Knightley. They have long
known each other, and he has long been in effect and in
fact (as her brother-in-law) one of the family. When she
imagines he might marry Harriet, her wish is rather that
things should remain as they always have been: 'Let
Donwell and Hartfield lose none of their precious intercourse of friendship and confidence, and her peace would
be fully secured' (416). Such a wish represents, in part, her
withdrawing herself from the idea of marriage. Interest-

ingly, she has both disclaimed any intention of marrying herself ('even if she were asked by Mr. Knightley'), and taken the view that he himself must never marry. Yet Emma's wish to have their 'precious intercourse of friendship and confidence' continue also indicates her almost subliminal recognition of what needs to develop further between them. She thinks in terms of Donwell and Hartfield, but ultimately must come to acknowledge what exists between them as people.

One cannot miss the genuine feeling that flows through so many of Emma's exchanges with Knightley, even if she is for so long unable to name it to herself for what it is. At the ball, when she offers to dance with him, she says, 'You have shown that you can dance, and you know we are not really so much brother and sister as to make it at all improper.' At this point the distinction between friendship and love (or the familial and the more nearly intimate) seems to disappear: 'Brother and sister!' he exclaims; 'no, indeed' (331). Another memorable instance is his taking her hand after learning of her visit to Miss Bates:

> He looked at her with a glow of regard. She was warmly gratified – and in another moment still more so, by a little movement of more than common friendliness on his part. – He took her hand; – whether she had not herself made the first motion, she could not say – she might, perhaps, have rather offered it – but he took her hand, pressed it, and certainly was on the point of carrying it to his lips – when, from some fancy or other, he suddenly let it go. – Why he should feel such a scruple, why he should change his mind when it was all but done, she could not perceive. – He would have judged better, she thought, if he had not stopped (385–6).

Knightley stops because he still has to learn the truth about her feelings for Frank. Especially interesting, however, is her consciousness of this seemingly natural and involuntary act. If what prompts it is not as yet part of her conscious mind, her thoughts anticipate that which, prompted by other circumstances, she will soon acknowledge to herself. Until being 'threatened with its loss, Emma had never known how much of her happiness depended on being *first* with Mr. Knightley' (415), and she imagines the loss of this in terms of the company they have so long shared: 'Mr. Knightley to be no longer coming there for his evening comfort! – No longer walking in at all hours, as if ever willing to change his own home for their's! – How was it to be endured?' (422). It is nevertheless what they must both endure as a result of their special kind of friendship that significantly provides the means of their coming together. Answering his task in speaking about her behaviour to Miss Bates on Box Hill is her resolve to take another turn in the garden and hear him out even though she expects to be told of his love for Harriet. But it is not 'as a friend' (429) – a phrase twice repeated – that Knightley wishes to speak to her, and her struggle to be selfless is rewarded by hearing him declare instead his love for her.

When he has spoken and she has accepted him, a new feeling suffuses the common pleasures that have always been theirs to enjoy:

> They sat down to tea – the same party round the same table – how often it had been collected! – and how often had her eyes fallen on the same shrubs in the lawn, and observed the same beautiful effect of the western sun! – But never in such a state of spirits, never in anything like it; and it was with difficulty that she could summon enough of her usual self to be the attentive lady of the house, or even the attentive daughter (434).

This everyday occurrence becomes invested with a new significance. It functions as a correlative of something important and enduring, the new radiance that surrounds it being suffused with a new and deeper kind of affection:

> What totally different feelings did Emma take back into the house from what she had brought out! . . . She was now in an exquisite flutter of happiness, and such happiness moreover as she believed must still be greater when the flutter should have passed away (434).

Subsequently Emma is inclined to doubt whether her 'own sense would have corrected' her without his 'assistance' (462), though Knightley modestly and magnanimously denies having helped. In a sense he is both right and wrong, as she is too. Through herself and her former mistakes she comes to know herself. And she comes to know herself through her love for him. It is said that 'the wishes, the hopes, the confidence, the predictions of the small band of true friends who witnessed the ceremony' of their marriage 'were fully answered in the perfect happiness of the union' (484). Yet such assurance is really unnecessary, given what we see of Emma and Knightley in the months before their marriage. Their life together promises not merely mutual trust but a great deal of liveliness between them. Emma herself never appears more animated than on hearing of the proposed marriage between Harriet and Robert Martin: 'She was in dancing, singing, exclaiming spirits; and till she had moved about, and talked to herself, and laughed and reflected, she could be fit for nothing rational' (475). Knightley, too, seems to blossom in their conversations together, the latent animation of his character responding delightedly to her playfulness. Having heard that Harriet has accepted Robert Martin, Emma appears to be somewhat incredulous:

> 'But, Mr. Knightley, are you perfectly sure that she has absolutely and downright *accepted* him. I could suppose

she might in time – but can she already? – Did not you
misunderstand him? – You were both talking of other
things; of business, shows of cattle, or new drills – and
might not you, in the confusion of so many subjects,
mistake him? – It was not Harriet's hand that he was
certain of – it was the dimensions of some famous
ox. . . .'

'Do you dare say this?' cried Mr. Knightley. 'Do you
dare to suppose me so great a blockhead, as not to know
what a man is talking of? – What do you deserve?

'Oh! I always deserve the best treatment, because I
never put up with any other.' (473, 474).

There is a marked difference between this and the
conversation of the novel's first chapter. While Emma
there spoke 'playfully' (10), she was forced to counter
Knightley with another kind of wit, to laugh off his words
as 'all a joke'. Yet the joking here, at the end of the novel,
is very different. Building, as it does, on their mutually
shared recognition of each other, it constitutes affectionate
teasing. The same spirit informs her response to John
Knightley's letter, when she remarks to her fiancé that his
brother 'is not without hope of my growing, in time, as
worthy of your affection, as you think me already' (464).
This kind of intimacy is neither cloying nor edged with a
degree of defensiveness. Though Emma had earlier said of
her relationship with Knightley, 'We always can say what
we like to one another', these are words which now
contain much more than a half-truth.

Anne Elliot

Persuasion lives as a novel through the thoughts and feelings of its heroine Anne Elliot. Yet in its first chapters she seems almost dismissed from notice during the account of her family's declining fortunes. Her father Sir Walter Elliot and her elder sister Elizabeth are both seen to be consumed by a sense of self, while Mary, her younger sister, is given to complaining and hypochondria, to a strain of selfishness sufficiently peevish. By these members of her family Anne is virtually ignored, except when she can be a convenience to them; 'she was only Anne' (5) – though of obvious use in playing at dances or nursing sick children. In her virtual exclusion from her family's vain and trivial world, she does, however, draw our interest. As well as having 'an elegance of mind and sweetness of character, which must have placed her high with any people of real understanding' (5), her very consciousness seems somehow suffused through the writing.[1] Her consciousness, indeed, is almost tangibly present because of her silent and continuing love for the previously rejected Captain Wentworth. His unique hold on her affections has only deepened her sense of loss, and over eight long years has consolidated in her a mind that is a 'whole complex unity' of thinking, feeling and action.[2] A far more sophisticated yet more retiring heroine than Catherine Morland – one who would have been a favourite sister to Elinor or Fanny, or have appreciated the real worth of Elizabeth or Emma – Anne is once again put in touch with Wentworth through pure chance. Yet the reader is made aware that between them there exists a peculiarly vibrant responsiveness, of which the power is obvious even though circumstances and the legacy of former feelings conspire in different ways to keep them apart.

In alluding to Anne's earlier engagement to Wentworth, the author remarks, 'Half the sum of attraction, on either side, might have been enough, for he had nothing to do, and she had hardly any body to love' (26). Anne was nevertheless persuaded to give him up by her friend Lady Russell, and what this cost both her and Wentworth is clear from the following passage:

> Had she not imagined herself consulting his good, even more than her own, she could hardly have given him up. – The belief of being prudent, and self-denying principally for *his* advantage, was her chief consolation, under the misery of a parting – a final parting; and every consolation was required, for she had to encounter all the additional pain of opinions, on his side, totally unconvinced and unbending, and of his feeling himself ill-used by so forced a relinquishment (28).

Accordingly, when they unexpectedly meet again at Uppercross Cottage, she is agitated and feels acute embarrassment:

> A thousand feelings rushed on Anne, of which this was the most consoling, that it would soon be over. And it was soon over. In two minutes after Charles's prep-aration, the others appeared; they were in the drawing-room. Her eye half met Captain Wentworth's; a bow, a curtsey passed; she heard his voice – he talked to Mary, said all that was right; said something to the Miss Musgroves, enough to mark an easy footing: the room

seemed full – full of persons and voices – but a few minutes ended it. Charles shewed himself at the window, all was ready, their visitor had bowed and was gone (59).

This scene is not merely pictured through Anne's eyes; its significance is felt through her very fibres. The space around her seems to collapse, and her impression is of 'persons and voices' that fill the room and crowd in upon her. Because of their long estrangement, she and Wentworth can no longer occupy the kind of shared space or privacy that presumably marked their earlier intimacy. Nor can she feel in the least confident that he would be willing to have this re-established. Even though she finds that 'to retentive feelings eight years may be little more than nothing' (60), she is unsure how 'his sentiments' are to be read. 'Was this like wishing to avoid her? And the next moment she was hating herself for the folly which asked the question' (60).

Wentworth could not at this time have accurately answered the question about his own feelings towards Anne. After he has met her again at the Cottage, he indulges what he later describes as 'those earlier feelings which I had been smarting under year after year' (245):

He had thought her wretchedly altered, and, in the first moment of appeal, had spoken as he felt. He had not forgiven Anne Elliot. She had used him ill; deserted and disappointed him. . . . She had given him up to oblige others. It had been the effect of over-persuasion. It had been weakness and timidity. . . . Except from some natural sensation of curiosity, he had no desire of meeting her again. Her power with him was gone for ever (61).

Though this is written in the third person, it clearly voices the substance of Wentworth's sentiments. And given that he feels this, we sense how great is the distance that separates him from Anne. We may detect in his definiteness a hint of something like self-defensiveness, as though he needs to assure himself of his conviction that she now means nothing to him. Yet what separates them is in one sense no less real for that, and the reader is left wondering what turn of events could possibly bring them together, and even, perhaps, whether their estrangement will not in the end prove final.

That we feel so keenly for Anne is coloured by this apparently incipient probability.[3] She is in no position to discuss her feelings with Wentworth or defend her earlier action both because she is a woman and because it was she who had originally broken off the engagement. Nor can she indulge in any pointed hinting; we have already been told of 'the nice tone of her mind, the fastidiousness of her taste' (28). *Persuasion* highlights the difficulty of communication where circumstances and feelings keep two people apart, and the effect of this is to make Anne's isolation seem even more intense – to give us a sense of how intensely lived it is. Being obliged to keep her deepest feelings to herself, she needs to practise a great deal of self-control, not merely to avoid any awkwardness, but to try to protect herself from even greater hurt. We enter into her plight, the more so given the self-possessed way she tries to cope with it. Immediately after meeting Wentworth again, she begins 'to reason with herself', and tries to will herself into such a state; yet we are also aware how empty any presumed conviction really is:

> 'So altered that he should not have known her again!'
> These were words which could not but dwell with her.
> Yet she soon began to rejoice that she had heard them.
> They were of sobering tendency; they allayed agitation;
> they composed, and consequently must make her
> happier (61).

While this overstates the degree of composure she has reached, Anne has (like Elinor Dashwood) a finely discriminating intelligence and is able to draw on impressive reserves of character. Though not foolish enough to think that the inevitable 'recollection' of 'former times' (produced by their being together) will lead to the renewal of his 'former feelings' (63), she is able to acknowledge to herself that she has 'seen the same Frederick Wentworth', 'not altered, or not for the worse' (61). In still responding to him in this way, Anne shows both her impressive selflessness and the depth of her own feelings. As Juliet McMaster has pointed out, there is a 'particular pain' for Anne in what is left of their long-lapsed intimacy[4] – a peculiar attentiveness which Anne tries to guard herself against but which makes her, even so, keenly observant of Wentworth. Moreover, though Wentworth's initial behaviour towards her virtually extinguishes all sense of hope, the reader can detect more in this than Anne is disposed, or can allow herself, to admit. When she comes near to the piano and he is sitting there, she finds 'his cold politeness, his ceremonious grace . . . worse than any thing' (72). Again, when he lifts the troublesome Walter Musgrove off her back, the noise he makes 'with the child' is interpreted by her to mean that he wished 'to avoid hearing her thanks, and rather sought to testify that her conversation was the last of his wants' (80). Wentworth (as we can see) is, despite himself, being drawn towards Anne, and his loss of 'composure' (79) when he unexpectedly finds himself alone with her may be taken as further evidence of his continuing interest in her.

That Anne is more certain than Wentworth of her own deeper feelings can be inferred from her degree of empathy for the temporarily slighted Charles Hayter, or her sense of being older 'in feeling' (97) than the self-indulgently sorrowing Captain Benwick. Though not daring to admit it to herself (because circumstances seem so much against her), she knows that Wentworth is not in love with either Henrietta or Louisa Musgrove; whereas he himself is bent on shaping the self-professedly decisive Louisa into the fancied image of what has hitherto been denied him in his unrealised love for Anne. It is a seemingly autumnal heroine that again meets him, and the suggestive use of seasonal details blends with the November walk at Uppercross when she remembers 'some tender sonnet, fraught with the apt analogy of the declining year, with declining happiness, and the images of youth and hope, and spring, all gone together' (85). Yet Anne has within herself the almost unconscious means of renewal. Her nature remains unblighted, and if she is not like 'the farmer . . . meaning to have spring again', she is able to counteract 'the sweets of poetical despondence' by calling on inner reserves of character. Though there is nothing purposive about her behaviour, hers is an inner generosity or magnanimity that ensures her ability to be responsive. Self-possessed in an unthrusting sense, and content to remain in the background without losing herself in feelings of self-indulgence, Anne is nevertheless sensitive to claims outside her own, and able to benefit in an unpresuming way from whatever kindles a corresponding spark in others.

When, during the walk at Uppercross, Anne overhears herself being discussed by Louisa and Wentworth, she detects 'just that degree of feeling and curiosity about her in his manner, which must give her extreme agitation' (89). Just prior to this, Wentworth has said to Louisa, 'It is the worst evil of too yielding and indecisive a character, that no influence over it can be depended on' (88). Yet his identification of a firm decisive character with the resilience of a hazelnut that 'has outlived all the storms of autumn', while revealing the bitterness of the sense of hurt he is still feeling, suggests his unconscious apprehension of a strength of character that is undeniably

Anne's. It is her avowal of the enduring quality of a woman's love that later so strikes Wentworth, and it becomes true that Anne, 'blessed with original strength', outlives 'all the storms of autumn'. At Lyme, when her looks have been heightened by a walk on the sands, and noticed with obvious approval by a passing gentleman (Sir Walter's heir William Elliot), Captain Wentworth gives her 'a glance of brightness, which seemed to say, "That man is struck with you, – and even I, at this moment, see something like Anne Elliot again"' (104). It takes, however, the more sensational and far-reaching incident of Louisa's fall on the Lower Cobb effectively to bring home to Wentworth Anne's true worth; in the ensuing confusion, she is the only one who does not lose her presence of mind. While his full appreciation of this is not learnt until much later, when he can speak to her about it he acknowledges that, as a result of what happened at Lyme, he 'learnt to distinguish between . . . the darings of heedlessness and the resolution of a collected mind' (242).

During the crisis itself, we glimpse not only how important to him is Anne's self-possession, but how integral a part it is of her own make-up:

> Anne, attending with all the strength and zeal, and thought, which instinct supplied, to Henrietta, still tried, at intervals, to suggest comfort to the others, tried to quiet Mary, to animate Charles, to assuage the feelings of Captain Wentworth (111).

Wentworth proposes that she stay behind with Louisa at the Harvilles':

> 'You will stay, I am sure; you will stay and nurse her;' cried he, turning to her and speaking with a glow, and yet a gentleness, which seemed almost restoring the past. – She coloured deeply; and he recollected himself, and moved away (114).

More than ever it is not in his power to approach re-establishing what has previously existed between them: given Louisa's injury, he is implicitly committed to her. His brief response to Anne nevertheless brings her to respond to him, even though within understood limits; yet her own pleasure on the occasion is almost immediately crossed by her 'mortifying reception' (116) when he learns that Mary, who has pushed her 'jealous and ill-judging claims' (115), is to stay behind instead of Anne. His reaction seems to proceed not so much from his disappointment that one sister has been substituted for another, as from a continuing sense that Anne has somehow let him down: 'She would have attended on Louisa with a zeal above the common claims of regard, for his sake; and she hoped he would not long be so unjust as to suppose she would shrink unnecessarily from the office of a friend.' During the drive back to Uppercross, his 'governing principle' seems to be 'to spare Henrietta from agitation', and when she laments 'the last ill-judged, ill-fated walk to the Cobb', he exclaims, 'Had I done as I ought! But so eager and so resolute! Dear, sweet Louisa!' Even so, Anne cannot help wondering whether he still persists 'in his own previous opinion as to the universal felicity and advantage of firmness of character' (as opposed to the virtue of a properly 'persuadable temper'), and his appeal to her concerning the best way to break the news to Louisa's parents amounts to a 'deference for her judgment' (117) which, even in parting from him, she is conscious of as 'a great pleasure'.

This move towards some renewed process of sharing is therefore crossed by circumstances, the first volume of the novel ending with Anne almost completely unaware of the effect she has once again had on Wentworth, while he himself has yet to realise the full force of it. She nevertheless comes to prize the little that has passed between them, 'some instances of relenting feeling, some

breathings of friendship and reconciliation, which could
never be looked for again, and which could never cease to
be dear' (123). Yet it is, she feels, only memories she has to
live on, even though her feelings are so strong that she
needs to try to cope with them by exorcising Captain
Wentworth, at least in name, before she can converse
about Lyme with apparent equanimity:

> She could not speak the name, and look straight forward
> to Lady Russell's eye, till she had adopted the expedient
> of telling her briefly what she thought of the attachment
> between him and Louisa. When this was told, his name
> distressed her no longer (124–5).

The intensity of Anne's feeling for Wentworth is captured
in such a passage. Though the pleasure of remembering
him is increased when the Crofts tell her of his appreciation of her 'exertions' (126) at Lyme, this cannot lead her
to hope. She does not feel a prospect of greater happiness.
What she feels exists only as memories.

Anne's is not, however, a vicarious experience for she
cherishes those memories which engage with real feelings.
Consequently, though William Elliot soon gives himself a
handsome introduction to the story, he can never be a
substitute lover for Wentworth. While the author at a
crucial stage fails to offer more than empty banalities in
trying to objectify Anne's consciousness of herself as well
as her devotion to Wentworth – 'Prettier musings of high-
wrought love and eternal constancy, could never have
passed along the streets of Bath' (192) – the reader is invited
to discern that Elliot is not the kind of man who could ever
replace Wentworth in her affections. This is evident, not
merely from what is known of Anne, but from what is
detected in Elliot's behaviour. At Lyme, he looks at her
too admiringly, so that the author's parenthetical 'completely a gentleman in manner' (104) is, however faintly,
studied and undercutting. In Bath he so readily wins

general approval that Lady Russell's neat summary of his
virtues contains a hint of the glibness he himself possesses:
'Every thing united in him; good understanding, correct
opinions, knowledge of the world, and a warm heart'
(146). Lady Russell is convinced of his worth by his
'strong feelings of family-attachment and family-honour,
without pride or weakness', his living 'with the liberality
of a man of fortune, without display', and his judging 'for
himself in every thing essential, without defying public
opinion in any point of worldly decorum'. In her view he
would be the ideal partner for Anne, and she entertains the
hope of seeing her young friend married to him 'in
Kellynch church, in the course of the following autumn'
(161).

Such a marriage must have led, however, to a long
winter of unhappiness, and even though Anne is in no
position to formulate this to herself, she rejects the idea
almost as soon as it is mentioned. In an important sense
she is proof against Elliot's charms because of her love for
Wentworth; but she is not left to reject Lady Russell's
suggestion on these grounds alone. True, she feels a
momentary yet intense pleasure at it:

> For a few moments her imagination and her heart were
> bewitched. The idea of becoming what her mother had
> been; of having the precious name of 'Lady Elliot' first
> revived in herself; of being restored to Kellynch, calling
> it her home again, her home for ever, was a charm
> which she could not immediately resist (160).

But as soon as Anne's thoughts extend to Elliot, she is
herself again: 'It was not only that her feelings were still
adverse to any man save one; her judgment, on a serious
consideration of the possibilities of such a case, was against
Mr. Elliot.'

It is important for our judgment of Anne that she should
be seen to reject Elliot before Wentworth is free to re-enter

her life. Only in this way can Jane Austen demonstrat
true moral worth of her heroine – her fine discriminat
that she remains truly possessed in herself of what is
dearest to her, that she has both a heart and mind to reject
the plausibly meretricious, the merely fair-seeming.
Moreover, given the earlier influence on her (an influence
which is misinterpreted by Wentworth), it is important
that Anne should be seen to have an inner strength of
judgment independent of Lady Russell's opinions. This is
made very clear through the episode of Mr Elliot, who,
earlier in their acquaintance, had seemed to Anne very
similar in his overall discretion and manners to Lady
Russell herself (144). It is not merely a question of his
revealing his apparent regard for rank (a fact which
endears him to Lady Russell as well as Anne's own
family). It is, more importantly, a question of exposing
the basis of such a regard, of penetrating his exterior polish
and seeming discretion in order to come at the real man
beneath.

Whereas in Elliot Lady Russell finds 'the solid so fully
supporting the superficial', Anne finds that her cousin and
herself do not 'always think alike' (148). Though he tries
to establish a footing of intimacy with her (as in his hinted
criticism of the friendship between her father and Mrs
Clay), she finds his character curiously nebulous, and
therefore not such as her own can willingly meet. His
respect for 'rank and connexion' seems to her to be 'not
merely complaisance' but 'a liking to the cause', and his
definition of 'good company' (150) is very different from
hers. She takes it to be 'the company of clever, well-
informed people, who have a great deal of conversation',
and there is a faint hint of the plausible when Elliot quips
that that is not 'good company' but 'the best'. Anne sums
him up to Lady Russell as 'an exceedingly agreeable man'
(159), the reserve in her words escaping her friend. She
had tacitly compared his manners ('so exactly what they

ought to be, so polished, so easy, so particularly agreeable') with those of Captain Wentworth: 'They were not
the same, but they were, perhaps, equally good' (143).
The difference between the two men is implied in her
careful choice of words, and as she comes to know Elliot
her doubt is reinforced in these terms: 'Though they had
now been acquainted a month, she could not be satisfied
that she really knew his character . . . Who could answer
for the true sentiments of a clever, cautious man, grown
old enough to appreciate a fair character?' (160, 161). As
Anne reflects on Elliot, she notes his inability to be 'open',
to respond with spontaneity, and this leads her to doubt
his sincerity. Events, of course, prove her to be right, and
she learns the truth about him from her old schoolfriend
Mrs Smith. Yet she herself has been quick to notice that
Elliot is 'too generally agreeable' (161), that he manages
too easily to get on well with a whole range of different
people. Indeed, in his pursuit of expediency, he may be
said to have 'no character at all'.[5] Though he is seemingly
so correct, Anne can neither approach any footing of
intimacy with him, nor therefore feel herself capable of
responding to him.

After Anne has effectively rejected Elliot, there is a sense
of virtue rewarded on her being told of Benwick's
engagement to Louisa: 'It was almost too wonderful for
belief; and it was with the greatest effort that she could
remain in the room, preserve an air of calmness, and
answer the common questions of the moment' (165).
Anne's 'heart beat in spite of herself, and brought the
colour into her cheeks' (167); and with this quickening of
spirit comes a responsiveness so intense that she can
scarcely contain herself. On catching sight of Wentworth
walking down the street, 'for a few minutes she saw
nothing before her' (175) – until, that is, she 'scolded back
her senses'.

The scene at the concert is also highly charged. So much

is felt between Anne and Wentworth that they naturally find it difficult to be relaxed with each other. Not only is she pained by her family's reluctance to acknowledge him, but she still has to assure herself of his real feelings; whereas he needs to be assured in turn that Elliot is not a successful rival. Anne takes the initiative in speaking to him when he arrives, and, despite the initial awkwardness, he remains with her and soon becomes more animated: 'and presently with renewed spirit, with a little smile, a little glow, he said . . .' (181). Wentworth quickly touches important subjects, and both what he says of Louisa and how he would expect a man to feel who had lost someone like Fanny Harville lead Anne 'to breathe very quick, and feel an hundred things in a moment' (183).

Just, however, as a resolution might be expected, the action is complicated by a reference to Lyme that is open to misconstruction. Whereas Wentworth supposes that she must have a painful memory of the place, Anne, 'with a faint blush at some recollections', adds, 'Altogether my impressions of the place are very agreeable' (184). At this moment they are interrupted by the arrival of Lady Dalrymple's party, and he parts from her thinking that her blush has been occasioned by Elliot. Anne herself is unaware of this, and her animated looks during the concert (which can also be misinterpreted) are primarily from a consciousness of what Wentworth has said:

> All, all declared that he had a heart returning to her at least; that anger, resentment, avoidance, were no more; and that they were succeeded, not merely by friendship and regard, but by the tenderness of the past; yes, some share of the tenderness of the past. She could not contemplate the change as implying less. – He must love her (185–6).

Nevertheless, despite all Anne can do in trying to see

Wentworth again, she is monopolised by her cousin and surrounded by the others; and she even misses the opportunity of exchanging a distant glance with him: 'As her eyes fell on him, his seemed to be withdrawn from her. It had that appearance. It seemed as if she had been one moment too late' (188). Even when she does get a chance to place herself within speaking distance, Miss Carteret claims her attention. Again her purposes are crossed, for Wentworth makes 'a reserved yet hurried sort of farewell' (190), and is gone without her being able to do anything about it. The evening that had promised so much has turned out frustratingly. While she does not realise that her words have given him reason for jealousy, she nevertheless realises that he is jealous: 'How was the truth to reach him? How in all the peculiar disadvantages of their respective situations, would he ever learn her real sentiments?' (191).

The lovers seem as far from a resolution as ever, and when Anne next meets Wentworth at the White Hart, she fears 'from his looks, that the same unfortunate persuasion, which had hastened him away from the concert room, still governed. He did not seem to want to be near enough for conversation' (221). In the words that follow about Elliot, Wentworth is 'all attention, looking and listening with his whole soul' (224), and Anne seizes the opportunity afforded by her brother-in-law to show her indifference for the party proposed for the next evening. This draws Wentworth again to her side, and his reference to their long period of separation gives the reader confidence that nothing further will keep them apart. Still, however, Anne is crossed by circumstances and kept in a state of continuing anxiety somewhere between happiness and misery. First Henrietta proposes their going out, obliging Anne to move; then, after Sir Walter and his eldest daughter have arrived and Elizabeth has given her invitation to Wentworth, Mary whispers 'very audibly': 'I do not wonder Captain Wentworth is delighted! You see he cannot put the card out of his hand' (227). The 'contempt' with which this remark is received is instantly noticed by Anne, and she is left in a state of wearisome and painful suspense, constantly 'harassing herself in secret with the never-ending question' whether he will come to her family's party or not.

The tension that has existed between them is brilliantly sustained until the very moment of resolution. There has necessarily been a difference between what Anne and Wentworth have each felt from moment to moment, yet their latent willingness to respond to each other has been cruelly criss-crossed and frustrated by circumstances. As in previous chapters, they are in the penultimate chapter both together and apart, but in this chapter they come together because circumstances do not prevent their knowing in all honesty each other's feelings. Less powerful feelings might have been able to endure a more direct declaration, but between them communication must still be indirect enough to allow room for uncertainties to be resolved without bruising the feelings or endangering the integrity of each.

Though stationed in different parts of the room, each remains alert to the other with a special kind of vibrancy. When Mrs Croft replies to Mrs Musgrove by questioning the wisdom of entering into an engagement without the clear prospect of being able to marry, Anne, feeling the application of his sister's words 'in a nervous thrill all over her', sees Wentworth pause in his writing and give 'one quick, conscious look at her' (231). Soon Captain Harville invites her to join him by a window which, 'though nearer to Captain Wentworth's table', was 'not very near' (231–2). Again Harville introduces the subject of Benwick and his late sister, and this leads to a debate about constancy in love in which Anne can put from her heart the woman's view:

'We certainly do not forget you, so soon as you forget
us. It is, perhaps, our fate rather than our merit. We
cannot help ourselves. We live at home, quiet, confined,
and our feelings prey upon us. You are forced on
exertion. You have always a profession, pursuits,
business of some sort or other, to take you back into the
world immediately, and continual occupation and
change soon weaken impressions' (232).

Harville will not allow this, maintaining that men's
stronger bodies imply stronger feelings; but Anne makes
use of 'the same spirit of analogy' to suggest that, though
man is more robust, he is not 'longer-lived' (233) – which
supports her view of the retentiveness of a woman's
feelings. Acknowledging the hardships men must endure,
she says, 'with a faltering voice', 'It would be too hard
indeed . . . if woman's feelings were to be added to all
this.'

It is clear from 'a slight noise' in 'Captain Wentworth's
hitherto perfectly quiet division of the room' that he has
been able to catch what Anne has been saying; yet it is
equally clear that she herself does not think he could have
heard it. She is therefore able to speak unself-consciously
about a woman's feelings, the more so because she is
talking to somebody else and they are debating the
question in general. Yet there is no escaping the personal
substance of Anne's words, which dispel the kind of
misconstruction occasioned at the concert. She sums up
the woman's case with a particular resonance that confirms
the frustration and pain it has brought her: 'All the
privilege I claim for my own sex (it is not a very enviable
one, you need not covet it) is that of loving longest, when
existence or when hope is gone' (235).

Wentworth's hurried note is a master stroke of decorum
in continuing the indirectness of communication that has
been forced on Anne and himself. Only when they meet

afterwards in the street and enter 'the comparatively quiet and retired gravel-walk' (240) can the course of their affections be intimately dwelt on. Within the larger progress of the action, this period together is aesthetically satisfying: after the tension of past uncertainties, it provides a period of relaxed animation, when the two lovers can luxuriate over the past and give to former memories the kind of exquisite poignancy which leads to an increase of happiness and understanding:

> They returned again into the past, more exquisitely happy, perhaps, in their re-union, than when it had been first projected; more tender, more tried, more fixed in a knowledge of each other's character, truth, and attachment; more equal to act, more justified in acting (240–1).

Accompanying this period of intimacy, of shared privacy, is the implication that the former seasons of autumn and winter have given way to the signs of an early spring, since the groups by which they are surrounded are 'sauntering politicians, bustling house-keepers, flirting girls' and 'nursery maids and children' (241).

It has been suggested that in *Persuasion* one gets a change of direction, even a new departure, in Jane Austen's work. Virginia Woolf, for example, has observed that in her last novel the author 'is beginning to discover that the world is larger, more mysterious, and more romantic than she had supposed'.[6] The apparent influence of the Romantic poets has been cited as a reason for this; though the figure of Benwick cautions against any over-indulgence in emotion purely for its own sake. During the walk at Uppercross, while Anne has present to her mind 'some few of the thousand poetical descriptions of autumn' (84), less inspiring aspects of the scene, like the description of Winthrop itself, 'without beauty and without dignity' (85), co-exist with the 'large enclosures, where the ploughs at work, and the fresh-made path spoke the farmer . . . meaning to have spring again'. The 'gradual ascent' they take through these enclosures anticipates Wentworth and Anne's later 'gradual ascent' (241) of the gravel walk in Bath, except that the hedgerows allow Anne only an embarrassed privacy to overhear Wentworth express again his pre-occupation with the dangers of indecision. This earlier sense of space offers the very opposite of freedom to each of the characters. On the gravel walk, however, while they are both 'heedless' of the varied activity that surrounds them, the author carefully notes this in a way that serves to highlight their renewed intimacy. The space they come to occupy is a space they occupy together. For this reason it is not merely enlarging rather than restrict-ing; it also provides a solid bulwark against this novel's seemingly wider view of potential occurrences.

The suggestion that, 'in sharp contrast with Jane Austen's other novels, we are left with no stable place or home in which we can imagine Anne's future happiness'[7] may therefore somewhat obscure what *Persuasion* endorses, The renewed intimacy between the heroine and her lover not only reminds us of the earlier novels, but confirms the central importance Jane Austen gives to the process of mutual sharing in human relationships. This is something which here transcends a conventional social context, though it does not negate social contexts of another kind. Looking back on what Wentworth (had she not refused him) would have been able to offer her, Anne notes during the evening she spends with his naval friends at Lyme that 'these would have been all my friends' (98). Though not offering the kind of security provided by a country mansion or a settled home, such characters would, as she clearly sees, have extended to her a far more positive and attractive alternative than anything she had previously encountered.

The original cause of Wentworth's resentment, Anne's

former submission to the judgment of Lady Russell, she herself examines and explains. 'If I had done otherwise,' she says, 'I should have suffered more in continuing the engagement than I did even in giving it up, because I should have suffered in my conscience' (246). Since she was only nineteen at the time, Lady Russell was then to her 'in the place of a parent'. We learn from the very first page of the novel that Anne was born in 1787. While she was not therefore at liberty to take her own decision, she decisively indicates that had Wentworth asked her 'in the year eight' (247) she would have renewed the engagement (that being the year in which she came of age). He can only regret his pride in not asking again; nevertheless, his strict and uncompromising examination of his previous conduct at least allows him to acknowledge the 'resolution' of Anne's 'collected mind' (242). Each may be said to have qualities of mind and heart that match the other's, yet there is, beyond this, an intimation of what they will come to enjoy and mean to each other in the very process of sharing such privacies. Theirs is indeed a process of sharing that will extend into the future. Significantly, Anne and Wentworth make use of 'the present hour' by giving it 'all the immortality which the happiest recollections of their own future lives' will 'bestow' (240). And because they engage in sharing what is 'so poignant and so ceaseless in interest' (241), the reader knows what the lovers themselves so surely know – that 'of yesterday and to-day there could scarcely be an end'.

Notes

INTRODUCTION

1 'Afterword' to *Northanger Abbey*, New York, New American Library, 1965, p. 213.

2 'Jane Austen', in *Jane Austen: A Collection of Critical Essays*, Ian Watt (ed.), Englewood Cliffs, New Jersey, Prentice-Hall, 1963, p. 15, note.

3 Valerie Shaw, 'Jane Austen's subdued heroines', *Nineteenth-Century Fiction*, vol. 30, no. 3, 1975, p. 282.

4 F. R. Hart, 'The spaces of privacy: Jane Austen', *Nineteenth-Century Fiction*, vol. 30, no. 3, 1975, p. 306, notes Jane Austen's 'urgent sense of true and false intimacy' and quotes J. C. Raines, *Attack on Privacy*, Valley Forge, New York, Judson Press, 1974, p. 55: 'Intimacy is the sharing of privacies.'

5 A. Walton Litz, '"A development of self": character and personality in Jane Austen's fiction', in *Jane Austen's Achievement*, Juliet McMaster (ed.), London, Macmillan, 1976, p. 68.

6 Juliet McMaster, *Jane Austen on Love*, Victoria, British Columbia, University of Victoria (ELS monograph series, no. 13), 1978, p. 60; but cf. also p. 78 where the author, quoting Donne's 'The Extasie', shows an even finer sense of what 'interinanimates' two souls.

7 Margaret Kirkham, *Jane Austen: Feminism and Fiction*, Sussex, Harvester Press, 1983, p. 40.

8 *Biographia Literaria*, ch. 14.

9 S. C. Burchell, 'Jane Austen: the theme of isolation', *Nineteenth-Century Fiction*, vol. 10, no. 2, 1955, p. 146.

10 Cf. Iris Murdoch's claim that 'only the very greatest art invigorates without consoling'; see 'Against dryness: a polemical sketch', in *The English Novel*, Stephen Hazell (ed.), London, Macmillan, 1978, p. 226.

11 *Solitude and Society*, trans. George Reavey, London, Geoffrey Bles, 1938, p. 89.
12 *Sense and Sensibility*, p. 364, and see below, p. 35.
13 *The Fear of Freedom*, London, Routledge & Kegan Paul, 1942, p. 98.
14 'Apropos Lady Chatterley's Lover', in *Sex, Literature and Censorship*, H. T. Moore (ed.), London, Heinemann, 1955, p. 265.

CATHERINE MORLAND

1 Despite Charlotte Brontë's generally low opinion of Jane Austen, she herself might have learned from her the use that could be made of such teasing. Certainly something comparable occurs between Jane Eyre and Rochester.
2 Cf. above, p. xii.
3 *Heroines of Fiction*, (1901), in *Casebook 2*, p. 57.
4 Ibid., and Marvin Mudrick, *Jane Austen: Irony as Defense and Discovery* (1952), in *Casebook 2*, pp. 55, 88.
5 Margaret Oliphant, *The Literary History of the Nineteenth Century* (1882), in *Casebook 2*, p. 53.
6 *North British Review* (1870), in *Jane Austen: The Critical Heritage*, B. C. Southam (ed.), London, Routledge & Kegan Paul, 1968, p. 244.
7 *Sincerity and Authenticity*, London, Oxford University Press, 1972, p. 82.
8 *On Liberty*, ch. 3.
9 Karl Kroeber observes that 'if Catherine sometimes misuses words, Henry sometimes misuses his senses'; 'Subverting a hypocrite lecteur', in *Jane Austen Today*, Joel Weinsheimer (ed.), Athens, Georgia University Press, 1975, p. 38. Cf. also Patricia Beer, *Reader, I Married Him*, London, Macmillan, 1974, p. 69.
10 *Casebook 2*, p. 92.
11 Cf. J. K. Mathison, '*Northanger Abbey* and Jane Austen's conception of the value of fiction', *Journal of English Literary History*, vol. 24, no. 2, 1957, esp. pp. 149–50.
12 Juliet McMaster has noted that 'Tilney needs Catherine just as she needs him'; 'Love and pedagogy', in *Jane Austen Today*, p. 70.
13 *Paradise Lost*, IV, 55–7.

Notes

Elinor Dashwood

1 *Quarterly Review* (1917), in *Casebook 1*, p. 88; cf. Marilyn Butler, *Jane Austen and the War of Ideas*, Oxford, Clarendon Press, 1975, p. 182, and Mudrick, *Casebook 1*, p. 89.
2 Ian Watt, 'On *Sense and Sensibility*', in *Jane Austen: A Collection of Critical Essays*, p. 48; David Cecil, *The Fine Art of Reading*, London, Constable, 1957, p. 117; Mona Wilson, *Jane Austen and Some Contemporaries*, London, Cresset Press, 1938, p. 6.
3 Cf. John Lauber, 'Jane Austen and the limits of freedom', *Ariel*, vol. 10, no. 4, 1979, p. 87 ('most readers have a bias toward feeling and freedom').
4 James McAuley, 'Celebration of love', *Under Aldebaran*, Melbourne, Melbourne University Press, 1946, ll. 83–5.
5 'Jane Austen and the limits of freedom', p. 86.
6 Cf. *Sense and Sensibility*, pp. 155, 180, 201, 211.
7 *Casebook 1*, p. 109.
8 Ibid., p. 104.
9 Ibid., p. 115.
10 Cf. Susan Morgan, 'Polite lies: the veiled heroine of *Sense and Sensibility*', *Nineteenth-Century Fiction*, vol. 31, no. 2, 1976, p. 191.

Elizabeth Bennet

1 Cf. H. S. Babb, *Jane Austen's Novels: The Fabric of Dialogue*, Ohio, Columbus, 1962, p. 127. Babb's analysis of the conversations between Darcy and Elizabeth is generally stimulating; see esp. pp. 125 ff.
2 *The Letters of the Earl of Chesterfield to His Son*, Charles Strachey (ed.), London, Methuen, 1901, vol. 1, p. 268.
3 Cf. Samuel Johnson, *Idler* 84: 'But if it be true which was said by a French prince, "that no man was a hero to the servants of his chamber", it is equally true that every man is yet less a hero to himself.'
4 J. P. Brown, *Jane Austen's Novels: Social Change and Literary Form*, Cambridge, Mass., Harvard University Press, 1979, p. 14.
5 B. C. Southam, Introduction, *Jane Austen*, London, Longman Group, 1975, p. 45, quoted by Brown, loc. cit.

Notes

FANNY PRICE

1 *Jane Austen's Novels: Social Change and Literary Form*, p. 81.
2 Opinions of *Mansfield Park* collected and transcribed by Jane Austen in *The Works of Jane Austen*, R. W. Chapman (ed.), vol. 6, and *Spectator* (1957), in *Casebook 1*, pp. 201, 246.
3 Cf. Lionel Trilling's sense of Mary Crawford's 'insincerity', *The Opposing Self* (1954), in *Casebook 1*, p. 227: 'Mary Crawford's intention is not to deceive the world but to comfort herself; she impersonates the woman she thinks she ought to be.'
4 *Jane Austen on Love*, p. 36.
5 Q. D. Leavis, Introduction to *Mansfield Park* (1957), in *Casebook 1*, p. 240.
6 *Casebook 1*, p. 204.
7 For an interesting discussion of the Mansfield theatricals, cf. Tony Tanner's Introduction, *Mansfield Park*, Harmondsworth, Penguin Books, 1966, pp. 27 ff.
8 'A portrait of Western man', *The Listener*, vol. 49, no. 1267, p. 970. Cf. also Trilling's discussion of the 'uncompromisingly categorical' nature of the judgments in *Mansfield Park* in *Sincerity and Authenticity*, pp. 77 ff.
9 Laurence Lerner, *The Truthtellers*, New York, Schocken Books, 1967, p. 160.
10 *Jane Austen's Novels: Social Change and Literary Form*, p. 86.
11 'The "irresponsibility" of Jane Austen', in *Critical Essays on Jane Austen*, B. C. Southam (ed.), Routledge & Kegan Paul, 1968, p. 18.

EMMA WOODHOUSE

1 J. E. Austen-Leigh, *Memoir of Jane Austen*, R. W. Chapman (ed.), Oxford, Clarendon Press, 1926, p. 157.
2 'The "irresponsibility" of Jane Austen', p. 6.
3 Cf. D. D. Devlin, *Jane Austen and Education*, London, Macmillan, 1975, p. 5.
4 Patricia Meyer Spacks, *The Female Imagination*, New York, A. A. Knopf, 1975, p. 124.
5 Lionel Trilling, 'Emma', *Encounter*, vol. 8, no. 6, 1957, p. 55.

6 Cf. A. M. Duckworth, *The Improvement of the Estate*, Baltimore, Johns Hopkins Press, 1971, ch. 4, esp. pp. 165 ff.
7 *Emma*, pp. 491–2.
8 'To Penshurst', ll. 1, 102.

ANNE ELLIOT

1 Cf. T. P. Wolfe, 'The achievement of *Persuasion*', *Studies in English Literature*, vol. 11, 1971, esp. pp. 688 ff.
2 Cf. Gilbert Ryle, 'Jane Austen and the moralists', in *Critical Essays on Jane Austen*, p. 121.
3 Cf. 'The "irresponsibility" of Jane Austen', p. 14; Ann Molan, 'Persuasion in *Persuasion*', *The Critical Review*, no. 22, 1982, p. 16.
4 Juliet McMaster, *Jane Austen on Love*, p. 72.
5 Pope's Epistle 'To a Lady', l.2.
6 *The Common Reader* (1925), in *Casebook 2*, p. 152.
7 Litz, '"A development of self": character and personality in Jane Austen's fiction', pp. 76–7.

Index of names